W9-AVJ-643

THE CHANNELING ZONE

THE CHANNELING ZONE

American Spirituality in an Anxious Age

MICHAEL F. BROWN

HARVARD UNIVERSITY PRESS

Cambridge, Massachusetts   London, England   1997

Library of Congress Cataloging-in-Publication Data
Brown, Michael F. (Michael Fobes), 1950–
    The channeling zone : American spirituality in an anxious
age / Michael F. Brown.
        p. cm.
    Includes bibliographical references and index.
    ISBN 0-674-10882-5
    1. Channeling (Spiritualism)—United States—History—20th
century.   2. Brown, Michael F. (Michael Fobes), 1950–
3. United States—Religion—1960– I. Title.
BF1286.B76   1997
133.9'1'0973—dc20   96-38375

CONTENTS

PREFACE

During the winter of 1989, I was one of several visiting anthropologists at the School of American Research, an institute for advanced study in Santa Fe, New Mexico. The snug adobe house provided by the School offered a view of the Sangre de Cristo and Jemez Mountains and the great sweep of sky between them. Standing on the patio at night to watch the unfamiliar western stars wheel overhead, I sometimes heard drumming from the house of my neighbor—not an American Indian, as it turned out, but an Anglo woman who regularly performed all-night healing rituals for friends and clients. Her impromptu ceremonies served notice that I had landed in an epicenter of the New Age, a diffuse social movement of people committed to pushing the boundaries of the self and bringing spirituality into everyday life. Although the term New Age is shunned by some, it accurately conveys the optimism and perceived urgency of their quest.

Ethnographic curiosity overpowered discretion, and I began to attend spirituality workshops at the Santa Fe Public Library and several of the town's personal-growth centers. Questions posed to people participating in these meetings evoked tales of vision quests and personal transformations that made the oral histories of the Amazonian Indians about whom I was then writing seem almost suburban by comparison. After several months of casual study, I began to take a more systematic look at the social and cultural dimensions of this flamboyant spiritual activity. Eventually my research interest narrowed to one of the most controversial expressions of alternative spirituality, channeling, which can be defined as the use of altered states of consciousness to contact spirits—or, as many of its practitioners say, to experience spiritual energy captured from other times and dimensions.

My journey into the world of channeling ultimately encompassed four years of episodic interviewing and approximately eight months of full-time research, including participation in workshops and weekend seminars. All told, I interviewed or observed forty practitioners of channeling and hundreds of ordinary people who attended channeling sessions for enlightenment or entertainment. Much of my fieldwork was conducted in the vicinity of Santa Fe, a town where urban cowboys from Houston belly up to the bar next to past-life regression therapists from Marin County. A mecca for artists and health-seekers since the early 1900s, Santa Fe is today one of the nation's foremost centers of alternative spirituality, much to the chagrin of the local American Indians and Hispanics, who find themselves pushed to the margins as the city experiences unprecedented growth. Like the smaller community of Sedona, Arizona, about 400 miles to the west, it has become a magnet for Americans in search of forms of spiritual understanding that they see as more authentic than those offered by mainstream religions.

For a broader perspective on channeling, I also explored my own backyard, western New England. In the eighteenth and nineteenth centuries, New England and upstate New York spawned many movements of religious renewal, ranging from the Great Awakenings of the 1740s and early 1800s to the utopian communes of the Shakers and the Oneida Community. Today the wellspring of American spiritual innovation has moved farther west. Nevertheless, New England offers an abundance of channeling workshops and counseling services which, while less exuberant than their New Mexican counterparts, still attract a diverse clientele. My investigation also took me on short trips to Arizona, California, Florida, New York, and Virginia.

In the pages that follow, I offer an assessment of channeling that tacks between the views of its advocates and my own first-hand observations at a range of channeling events. The latter presented special difficulties. In intimate workshop settings where it would have been impossible to remain a bystander taking notes in the corner, I faced the choice of either pretending to participate or actually throwing myself into the channeling experience as best I could. The second course proved simpler and more forthright. Participant-observation ultimately offered glimpses of the world behind channeling's public face: subtle struggles over spiritual turf, tensions between autonomy and dependence, conflicting notions of gender, vexing issues of money, and a lively sense of humor often absent from channeling books and magazines.

After months of involvement in the world of spirit communication, I came to the conclusion that most practitioners of channeling—who as a rule refer to themselves as "channels" in preference to the more familiar term "channelers"—are sincere in their beliefs and genuinely committed to spiritual growth as they understand it. Their commitment merits an analytical approach marked by the same combination of respect and detachment typically brought to research on the religions of Asia, Africa, and Latin America. Basic respect for others' beliefs does not preclude reflection on the *implications* of those beliefs, however. Channeling rests on a series of assumptions about the historical trajectory of human beings, both as individuals and as members of a community. Some of these assumptions are admirable, others disturbing. Together they hold a mirror to our society as it is experienced by the growing number of people who seek meaning in New Age practices.

Although this book offers a comprehensive view of contemporary spirit communication, some variations on the theme have doubtless escaped my attention. Market pressures force professional channels to innovate and diversify. Their restlessly shifting interests led me on brief excursions into other areas of alternative spirituality, including shamanism, energy work, goddess-centered religion, and the imitation of American Indian rituals, some of which are documented here.

When I began this research, academic colleagues frequently asked, "Why are you studying this?" Many found my interest in channels baffling and in subtle ways contaminating; like others who have studied controversial groups, I was suspected of having gone native. In contrast, channels themselves viewed the project as a stage in my own spiritual growth. A few conjectured that I would follow the lead of other rogue academics who found Western science too restrictive and eventually abandoned university positions for new careers as freelance writers, lecturers, or gurus. My loyalty to conventional methods of exposition may disappoint them.

They were right about one thing, however: many of my comfortable assumptions about shared understanding were shattered, probably never to be restored. I vividly recall documenting the life story of a bright and attractive woman whose spiritual path had brought her from Manhattan to New Mexico. She shared spellbinding tales of paranormal experiences and miracles that ranged from intergalactic voyages to an arduous apprenticeship with a Peruvian shaman. Although it was impossible to accept parts of her autobiography as literally true, I became convinced that her passionate sense of mission, which is shared by thousands of others engaged in similar religious explorations, could tell us something about the hopes and obsessions of our age. In the spirit of Alexis de Tocqueville's reflections on American democracy early in the nineteenth century, then, I have tried to illuminate a novel expression of American individualism and religiosity at the end of the twentieth.

The support of various institutions, friends, and loved ones made this work possible. Start-up funding was provided by Francis C. Oakley, then president of Williams College, who as a distinguished medieval historian might take satisfaction in knowing that his patronage represented a form of celestial intervention. In 1993, the School of American Research again offered me shelter in Santa Fe; I am especially grateful to the School's president, Douglas W. Schwartz, for his backing and encouragement. The Wenner-Gren Foundation for Anthropological Research, Inc., provided financial support at a critical point in my field research.

Many colleagues—far too many, unfortunately, to mention

by name—were kind enough to comment on individual chapters. Those who assessed drafts of the entire book include Jean Bacon, Sylvia Kennick Brown, Donna Chenail, Kai Erikson, Jim Howe, Bob Jackall, Bill Merrill, Molly Mullin, Francesca Polletta, Daniel Taub, Mark Taylor, Robin Waterfield, and Bob Woodbury. I am indebted to Joyce Seltzer, my editor at Harvard University Press, and to Gerard McCauley, my literary agent, for their support and wise counsel. My keen appreciation for the advice of these thoughtful readers in no way implicates them in the book's shortcomings.

Those who helped me navigate the spirit world were willing to remain anonymous, although some clearly would have preferred to receive credit for their ideas. While sympathetic to such concerns about intellectual property, I have honored the norms of contemporary social science by using pseudonyms and, in some cases, by relocating people to fictional places, thus preventing potential embarrassment to those who might regret certain confidences when they see them in print. When, as is often the case, spirits are closely identified with individual channels, I have invented new names for them as well. Only the identity of public figures remains unchanged. Among these are several celebrity channels whose controversial pronouncements have attracted national media attention.

Although I cannot thank my interlocutors by name, I trust that admiration for their infectious curiosity and gratitude for their openness are evident in the pages that follow. Some of them will disagree with my interpretations of channeling. Others may feel that the analysis focuses excessively on matters peripheral to spiritual growth. In reply, I would simply say that my goal has been to write a book that allows readers to reach conclusions quite different from my own.

My wife, Sylvia Kennick Brown, offered cheerful companionship on expeditions to channeling sessions and desert power-spots, where her sharp eye caught much that mine might have missed. She also endured stoically my habit of rising before dawn to wrestle with a writer's demons. For these indulgences, and many more, I owe her special thanks.

"Although the desire to acquire the good things of this world is the dominant passion among Americans, there are momentary respites when their souls seem suddenly to break the restraining bonds of matter and rush impetuously heavenward."

—Alexis de Tocqueville, *Democracy in America,* 1835

INTO THE CHANNELING ZONE

The worn rental tape yields a stippled video image of beige walls, potted palms, and two seated figures, a man and woman, deep in conversation. The woman, middle-aged and carefully groomed, responds to the man's questions. She gestures expressively as she speaks. Her restless hands, with their long, polished nails, resemble dancing starfish.

She is J. Z. Knight, arguably America's best-known practitioner of channeling. J. Z. became a celebrity by allowing her body to serve as a vehicle for Ramtha, The Enlightened One, an Atlantean warrior and deity whose voice emerges when she enters trance. Responding to a question about her life before Ramtha, J. Z. describes a world of suburban alienation in which nothing mattered more than dinner parties, hybrid roses, and her children's braces. In 1977 she was transformed by the sudden appearance of an enormous figure dressed in robes of light: Ramtha. There is no easy way to explain Ramtha's arrival at this time, J. Z. insists, because she had never heard of channeling or cults or even self-awareness. Ramtha appeared to her with steadily greater frequency. He read her thoughts and allayed her fears about his presence. After these encounters, she says, "I no longer belonged at social functions talking about Dior gowns and yeast infections and who's having an affair with whom."

As J. Z. summarizes Ramtha's message, her voice quavers and tears well up in her eyes. "Ramtha," she says, "allows us the vision, the hope, the desire to become all that we can become, which is unlimited probability. He will be remembered for teaching us how to love again realistically." She brushes away tears as the interviewer thanks her for sharing these experiences. It appears that the interview is over. Then, in a move of striking intimacy, she leans toward the interviewer, resting her hand lightly on the arm of his chair. She looks directly at him. "But you know something? What does it take for a person to make a mark on the consciousness of all people? Does it take suffering? Sacrifice? Does it take laying down one's life? Or does it take the courage to *live* that life?" She sits back and gazes demurely at the carpet. Her voice drops a notch in intensity. "I rather think that it takes the courage to live it. And in this little moment that we share this together, Les, one day, down the road, that courage is going to be remembered." He nods his head. She gazes at her hands as he thanks her. The interview ends.

The scene shifts to a hotel ballroom. J. Z. sits on a dais in a large wicker throne, bird of paradise plants framing her frosted hair. She wears white slacks and a loose white tunic trimmed in brilliant magenta. Her dazzling smile fills the center of the screen. She answers questions posed by members of the audience. One asks what it's like to channel Ramtha. "I'm in a different time-flow when I leave this body, because when I channel, I physically die. My spirit and soul and the essence that is

J. Z. completely gives up the body." Another asks her why Ramtha chose her as his vehicle. "Why not?" J. Z. replies. The audience that fills the large ballroom laughs, then applauds enthusiastically.

J. Z. explains that the people producing the video want to film her as she opens herself to Ramtha, a transition that usually takes place in private. Saying farewell, she reminds the audience that simply by being there, by witnessing, they make an important contribution to humanity. She blesses them, then settles into a lotus position in the wicker chair. The grainy videotape spools on soundlessly, showing nothing but the woman in the chair. Waiting out the uncomfortable silence, a viewer is simultaneously present and absent, caught up in real-time communion yet able to freeze, reverse, or fast-forward events at will.

J. Z.'s head drops. She breathes heavily. The camera view cuts to her right hand: the long nails, a gold band with large diamonds. Her head begins to rock. Slowly she brings up her arms until they are braced rigidly on the arms of the chair. Her feet drop to the floor, and she rises stiffly, hands balled into fists. She stamps her right foot, then her left. Gruffly, she shouts "Indeed!" to one side of the ballroom, then the other. Each time, the audience responds, "Indeed." Her eyes open. She begins a series of geometric movements: bowing to the chair behind her, lifting her arms, profiling her body to the camera. She moves to a man sitting in a chair to her right, evidently her husband. "Beloved Jeffrey, indeed how be you?" Bending to his hands, she kisses them noisily. "Be you that which is termed as it were indeed pleased to be here?" The strong, angular body movements and twisted syntax signal that she is now Ramtha. "Shall we get on with that which is termed as it were indeed barraging the masses, eh?" Laughter ripples through the audience.

She wanders off the dais and begins to work the crowd as Ramtha. She greets the cameraman, pats the sound technician on the head, and trades repartee with the director, who tries to steer her back toward a section of the ballroom with better lighting. The audience is delighted. J. Z. walks down the rows of chairs, touching various people whom she addresses as "entity" or "beloved one." The camera pans to a familiar face in the audience: Shirley MacLaine, the actress. People chuckle at Ramtha's humor, yet there is a deferential glint in their eyes as they track J. Z.'s movements.

She roams to the middle of the room and stops in front of a gray-haired man. "All the way here from the great country of Texas. Is your house still in order?" "It's still in order," the man drawls. She leans over to gaze into his eyes. It is the same sudden intimacy that transfigured the interview earlier on the tape. She tenderly caresses his face. The man looks serious and slightly uncomfortable. She strokes the back of his head. She retreats a step, putting her hands on his shoulders and peering at his face. "You talked of that which is termed your beloved's passing?" She takes hold of his hands. "There are that which is termed but a few things for you to do." He purses his lips. Again she caresses his face. "I'm going to bring you great joy. I want you to know what that is. And once leave you, entity, I'm going to take you to where I am, straightaway." "Great," he says. She kisses his hands again. She steps backward, pauses. Looking at him still, she lifts a forefinger: "I send you a comforter."[1]

For social critics, J. Z. Knight and her channeled deity, Ramtha, serve as icons of the New Age, a movement that one scholar of American religion has defined as a search for "the primal experience of transformation," both of the self and of society.[2] The philosophy outlined by Knight in her workshops, tapes, and videos is a volatile mixture of optimism and dark prophecy. The planet, Ramtha has said, will undergo apocalyptic changes—seismic and volcanic cataclysms, floods, and climatic shifts—that will propel us into a new era in which we can realize our true potential as gods. Although these predictions are taken seriously by some of Knight's followers, hundreds of whom have moved to the Pacific Northwest in search of places that Ramtha has deemed safe from catastrophe, most seem drawn to Knight's performances primarily by the promise of total self-fulfillment. When Knight experienced legal difficulties related to a bitter divorce in the early 1990s, the *New York Times* gave the story front-page coverage. Journalistic accounts detailed her financial empire, which was based on the millions that she earned from book sales and clients' fees, and speculated about whether Ramtha would be called to testify in court. In 1995 she again came to public attention when it was revealed that the Federal Aviation Administration paid $1.4 million for sensitivity training classes administered by one of her disciples.[3]

Although J. Z. Knight's highly publicized troubles have led some of her devotees to seek spiritual wisdom elsewhere, the notion that channeling is in decline could hardly be more mistaken. Just as the number of people joining evangelical Christian congregations increased despite the scandals that enveloped prominent televangelists, so the controversy surrounding Knight has failed to slow the quiet spread of channeling techniques to individuals willing to experiment with them at home. Today, workshops that teach people how to contact their spirit guides and guardian angels are offered at personal-growth centers around the nation. Those unable to attend channeling classes can easily turn to mass-market books that offer coaching in the best way to contact helpful spirits. In the nation's urban areas, psychotherapists discreetly use channeling to treat their clients' emotional distress.

Channeling, in other words, has moved from the gilded ashrams of the West Coast to the living rooms and offices of the American heartland. On the way, it has shed some of its sensational qualities in favor of a more muted approach to personal insight. It is now a well-established form of religious exploration that is likely to be with us for a while. Its practitioners believe that they can use altered states of consciousness to connect to wisdom emanating from the collective unconscious or even from other planets, dimensions, or historical eras. They apply their insights to financial affairs, career issues, relationships, and the resolution of emotional problems.[4] As practiced today, channeling incorporates features of nineteenth-century American spiritualism and a number of more recent influences, including the personal recovery movement and woman-centered spirituality.

Credible estimates for the number of Americans involved in channeling are hard to come by. At the height of media interest in channeling in the mid-1980s, one authority declared that a thousand channels practiced in the Los Angeles area alone. Even if this figure is an exaggeration, a surprising number of people accept the plausibility of communication with spirits. A Gallup poll conducted in 1994 revealed that more than 25 percent of Americans claim to believe in reincarnation and the possibility of communication with the dead, a substantial increase from a similar poll taken only a few years before. A national survey conducted by *Time* in 1993 found that 69 percent of adults accept the existence of angels; nearly a third of these had "felt an angelic presence" in their lives. Books written by prominent channels, including Jane Roberts, Edgar Cayce, and Helen

Schucman (the latter a psychologist who channeled the immensely popular *A Course in Miracles*) have enjoyed sales of a half-million copies or more, and most remain in print. Presumably, only a fraction of those who buy these works actually channel, but the books' continued popularity attests to public willingness to accept channeling as a valid source of insight. The diffusion of channeling to grassroots America is inseparable from the expansion of America's self-help business and the explosive growth in alternative health care, the latter now an industry that accounts for annual spending of $10–14 billion.[5] Citing estimates developed by sociologists at the University of California–Santa Barbara, Michael D'Antonio declares that 12 million Americans actively participate in New Age activities and another 30 million may be more peripherally involved.[6]

Americans who become involved in so-called New Religious Movements (NRMs) such as channeling stand near the top of the nation's households with respect to income and educational attainment. A disproportionate number are Baby Boomers, members of the large cohort of Americans born between 1946 and 1964. Baby Boomers attracted to NRMs are better educated but slightly less affluent than their cohort as a whole. Although the majority hold white-collar jobs, the frequency with which they change residences, jobs, and friends suggests that they have more unsettled lives than other Boomers.[7]

People involved specifically in channeling fit the general profile of Boomers who find their way into other NRMs. There is, however, a significant demographic split between the producers and the consumers of channeled information. The consumers—those who attend channeling workshops or seek individual counseling from channels—are well educated and often affluent. Channels—the producers in this exchange—have educational backgrounds similar to their clients, but their economic situation is often precarious because of their unusual career. Some channels use channeling as their primary means of income. Others have ordinary jobs and try to fit channeling activities into their free time. The professional channels who enjoy the most stable incomes are those who manage to integrate channeling into a conventional occupation, often as psychotherapists or motivational trainers.

Although outsiders are predisposed to view those drawn to channeling as emotionally unstable or, at the very least, conspicuously eccentric, most succeed in weaving their unusual gift into the fabric of lives that are otherwise fairly conventional. They hold jobs, dress presentably, establish stable loving relationships, and pay their taxes. Their stories may express a certain restlessness here or an idiosyncratic turn of the imagination there, but channels have no monopoly on these characteristics.

Still, channeling remains a fringe practice even by the tolerant standards of alternative spirituality, and people with direct exposure to it probably number in the hundreds of thousands rather than in the millions. Small numbers may carry great social weight, however. Given the ease with which ideas diffuse in mass society, unorthodox beliefs open a philosophical space that lends plausibility to views once regarded as odd or threatening. Channeling represents a frontier outpost in the shadow of which more popular expressions of New Age spirituality—goddess worship, meditation, inner-child work, and various forms of alternative healing—can prosper. And although the concepts that underlie channeling may be unconventional, its practitioners are overwhelmingly educated and middle-class, a fact that greatly magnifies its cultural impact. The people involved in channeling are a philosophical vanguard for ideas that now make their way into self-help programs, support groups, and the clinical orthodoxy of American health care.

When new developments in alternative spirituality come to the attention of the general public, it is usually because a journalist has seen them as an opportunity to practice the art of high irony. The print and electronic media can be counted on to serve up the latest example of transcendental silliness: the woman who channels the spirit of her clients' Barbie dolls for a fee of $3, for instance, or a channeled conversation with Babe Ruth about his role in otherworldly exhibition games.[8] In the mid-1980s, the cartoonist Gary Trudeau entertained readers of *Doonesbury* with a story line that featured a channeled 21,000-year-old warrior named Hunk-Ra, an obvious send-up of J. Z. Knight's spirit ally, Ramtha. The apogee of press interest in channeling may have been reached in 1996, when it was revealed that the First Lady, Hillary Rodham Clinton, had engaged in imaginary conversations with Eleanor Roosevelt and Mahatma Gandhi under the guidance of the New Age psychotherapist Jean Houston. Critics of the Clinton administration immediately concluded that the President's wife had "experimented with channeling" in the hallowed precincts of the White House, although nothing of the kind seems actually to have taken place. Whatever the truth of the matter, it was a field day for the media.

Intellectual circles, in contrast, seem wary of the New Age, and academic studies of alternative spirituality, especially ones based on first-hand experience, are surprisingly scarce. After hearing about my research, for example, a psychologist remarked, "I don't know how you can spend time with these sickening New Age types. They're just rich people with too much time on their hands." Her opinion was only slightly more caustic than those offered by other university colleagues. None would think of making such disparaging comments about the religious beliefs of the Yoruba, the Hopi, or the Australian Aborigines. The cultural critic Andrew Ross observes that many of his fellow university professors, even those interested in popular culture, regard the New Age as "the lowest of the low." The academic mind, whether of the scientific or humanist persuasion, thrives on distinctions and particulars, whereas New Age thought seeks connections and universals, which are pursued with an enthusiastic holism that disorients thinkers trained in highly specialized disciplines. In those New Age practices that focus on self-improvement, critics see narcissism, political complacency, or victim-blaming. This hostile response may also reflect the similarities, as much as the differences, between New Age ideology and contemporary academic work. The New Age, for instance, celebrates indeterminacy and moral relativism. It has also embraced the rhetoric of personal empowerment that characterizes writing in the humanities today. For many academics, the likeness may be too close for comfort.[9]

Yet close examination of channeling and related practices can reward the attentive observer. In common with forms of spirit mediumship practiced in many non-Western cultures and with the dramatic expressions of spiritual communication found among Christian pentecostalists closer to home, channeling offers an improvisational alternative to formal religious institutions. Mediums and channels bypass religious specialists to establish direct, personal contact with the spirit world. The messages that they find there reveal local concerns that have not yet breached the walls of institutionalized religion, which in its search for permanence tends to respond slowly to changing social conditions. Unburdened by rigid procedures, channeling operates close to the everyday experience of those who embrace it—their hopes, their troubles, and the language in which they frame their personal search for meaning. By attending to these experiences, we can learn much about their inner lives and the social forces that shape them.

Channeling also exhibits remarkable continuities with the now largely forgotten spiritualism of the nineteenth century, suggesting that its preoccupations reflect deep-seated aspects of the American character, not some sudden outburst of postmodern irrationality. In common with spiritualism, channeling is dominated by women who find in communication with spirits a refuge from mainline religions that even today offer little scope for their spiritual aspirations. Not only can female channels achieve the religious authority denied them elsewhere, they are free to embody male spirits or "energies" in ways that many find liberating. Increasingly, both men and women involved in channeling are drawn to androgynous spirits that have moved beyond gender altogether. The complex play of sexual identities evident in channeling offers unexpected insight into the emotional struggles of middle-class Americans as they try to survive the gender wars of our time.[10]

Criticism of the New Age and personal-growth movements often focuses on their fee-for-services character, which has sparked allegations of financial impropriety. From the perspective of channels and their clients, however, money is a morally neutral raw material, a view that they inherit from nineteenth-century self-help movements that promoted the power of positive thinking. Many, in fact, believe that market relations are more natural and democratic than those found in organized religious congregations. Their outlook sheds light on major changes in the attitudes of Americans toward their choice of religion, a decision increasingly based on a utilitarian assessment of personal needs rather than unwavering loyalty to the religion of their parents. It also has much to teach us about the extent to which every aspect of American life, including religion, has become a commodity. Certain channels aggressively protect their intellectual property—some, in fact, even seeking trademark status for their spirit guides—but their behavior simply emulates the behavior of corporate America, which now asserts ownership of everything from human gene sequences to the symbols that animate the imagination of our children.

Above all, channeling affords an ideal vantage from which to observe the mutability or fragmentation of the self that social philosophers have identified as a key feature of postmodern experience. The psychiatrist Robert Jay Lifton suggests that ours is the era of the "protean self," a time when personal identity is subject to constant reinvention.[11] In the course of a single day we may be required to adapt to wildly dissonant social worlds, taking on a different persona in each. For artists, actors, and advocates of computer-mediated communication, these opportunities to experiment with different identities are exhilarating, and they are likely to extol the creative possibilities of "decentered selves." Others, however, discover that they are less protean than the world demands and more decentered than their sense of emotional stability can sustain. The dramatic increase in the incidence of multiple personality since the 1980s is surely one index of the anxiety produced by self-decentering, as is the spread of forms of political and religious fundamentalism that offer adherents an unambiguous social identity.

Channels and their clients have elevated the protean impulse to a sacred principle. Their celebration of self-expansion invites a host of questions. How do people apparently not so different from the rest of us feel when they gaze in the mirror, perhaps while brushing their teeth, and think: "Good morning, Kal-El, fifth-dimensional alien being who has taken over the body of Brad Johnson," or "Here I am, Susan Blake, who in a previous lifetime was Nefertiti"? How do these ideas enhance their sense of themselves? How can they reconcile such exotic self-images with jobs, family responsibilities, and the other entanglements of ordinary life? Where do these desires come from, and how are they shaped by the cultural forces of our time? What does the steady diffusion of channeling into mainstream culture tell us about the future of religion in the United States?

Such questions, of course, skirt the issue of channeling's ultimate validity—that is, whether it represents a paranormal phenomenon defying scientific understanding. I recall a conversation with a psychologist who described his involvement with channeling, including participation in a seminar offered by J. Z. Knight nearly a decade before. He offered incisive criticism of Knight's sometimes overbearing style and the questionable financial dealings that eventually clouded her reputation. "But you know," he said, "when she put her hand on my head while channeling Ramtha, the energy was so powerful that I could barely handle it." "I don't know what she's doing now," he concluded, "but back then J. Z. really *had* something." His story was a gentle reminder that experience may have a magical quality that simply cannot answer to rational thought or argumentation.

Nevertheless, many channels exhibit only scant interest in debates about whether channeling is, or is not, a manifestation of the paranormal. Instead, their attitude is pragmatic. "I couldn't care less about where this information comes from or whether the beings that I channel are real," many insisted. "The only important thing is whether the information they provide is *true,* whether it makes my life better." With characteristic American practicality, they insist that these dramatic, sometimes uncanny, experiences, which may include encounters with angels, aliens, or Ascended Masters, have a positive effect on their relationships and careers. This willingness to suspend disbelief and open the self to messages from other places, other times, is the defining feature of the channeling zone.

2

LINKING UP

Ten people were gathered in a house in upstate New York to talk to Kana. A handout circulated by the organizers explained that Kana "lives on a future dimensional plane, parallel to ours but ahead of us by many thousands of years." Janet and Bud, the gathering's hosts, were a talkative couple in their late fifties or early sixties. The books piled on the shelves of their living room suggested eclectic interests: aeronautics, color therapy, electronics, Buddhism, paleontology. Outside the large kitchen window, songbirds plundered three feeders in the soft twilight of spring. When greetings had been exchanged and electronic recording equipment deployed next to the kitchen table, attention turned to the two men in charge of the evening's activities, Paul and Jack.

Paul, a studious-looking middle-aged man, was to serve as Kana's channel. His encounters with Kana began a decade ago, when he experienced a steadily intensifying series of dreams and psychic experiences that at first led him to fear for his sanity. Reassured by friends familiar with such phenomena, he eventually allowed the voices inside him to emerge. They came into focus as Kana, a being from the future. Over the ensuing years, the relationship between Paul and Kana deepened and became more comfortable.

Although Paul provided the critical link to Kana, the evening event was orchestrated by his friend Jack, who regularly handled the logistical side of Paul's performances. Jack had an expansive style, and with his high color, moustache, and generous girth, he looked the part of a jovial master of ceremonies. Like Paul, Jack had another life as a technician in the communications industry.

The people sitting around the table were a cross-section of the local suburbs. As far as one could tell by appearances, they were law-abiding middle-class citizens who could slip unnoticed through any shopping mall. The mood was light, and laughter echoed off the old beams of the kitchen as Paul settled down to enter the trance that activated his link to Kana.

Before the session began, Jack explained for the benefit of newcomers that Kana belongs to a society of future technocrats, survivors of a terrestrial holocaust that took place when human beings harnessed an apparently limitless power source that had the unanticipated effect of depleting the planet's gravitational energy. Billions died, spun off into space. The few survivors founded a society combining technological sophistication with ecological balance. A radical faction of these beings decided to contact contemporary humans—who are, of course, their ancestors—to warn them of the impending disaster and, if possible, to avert it. If they succeed, they will erase themselves from the future, a fate that they're willing to accept if they can prevent the destruction of human life as it currently exists.

Paul closed his eyes as Jack invited us to take some deep breaths. A moment later, Jack began his invocation: "Dear

Lord, we are gathered here in Thy name to quest and seek answers with this manifestation of truth, intelligence, and love.
Please locate this group." After several seconds of silence, he
asked, "Are you there?" Paul's voice answered in the affirma-
tive.

"Greetings," Jack said. "Are you Kana?"

"Yes."

Paul's channeling voice was labored and mechanical. He
linked words with a humming sound, as in "Magic is within the
mmm mind. If you allow mmm it to become part of you, mmm
it is." At Jack's prompting, Kana described the social organization of his community.

"We have one thought and mind. We share all feelings and
hearts and deeds. At present we share all postures of living. If
one has a problem, all share the problem and through our mass
dissipate it. Eventually we learned other sharing techniques, and
so we merged as a single unit." When asked why he has contacted us at this time, he said, "In the beginning, we sought to
learn. It was an inquisitive move."

The long-time members of the group, who had heard this before, looked impatient. At the first opportunity, they fired off
questions about the technology of Kana's society. Bob, a man in
his sixties who was clearly fascinated by technical details, badgered Kana for information about his people's energy source, a
device that focuses power from the planet's internal vibrations.
When Kana waffled, Bob expressed doubts about the accuracy of
his descriptions. The other old hands around the table occasionally cracked jokes at Kana's expense, and in his robotic way he
gave as good as he got. After Paul drew a humanoid face that represented an image of Kana's features, someone asked whether
the two triangles on the forehead were antennas. "No," Kana re-

sponded in his best interdimensional deadpan, "we have cable." A chorus of groans arose from the group.

After an hour and a half of these exchanges, the group was obviously tiring. Jack quietly brought the session to a close by thanking Kana and breaking off communication. Paul opened his eyes. During the entire session, he had been seated with his eyes closed, moving only to draw a few diagrams. He got up to stretch, and our hostess, Janet, bustled about the kitchen. As she passed around chips and salsa, members of the group spoke of the effects ten years of communication with Kana have had on their way of looking at the world. Although Janet didn't accept at face value everything that Kana revealed to them, she said that the experience of hearing Paul channel Kana had affected her life in positive ways. "You see, I deal with this information from an intuitive standpoint," she explained. "A lot of the philosophical sessions we've had with Kana have helped me to see that the things guiding me are the right things. These encounters teach us that our powers are far greater than we know. I'm amazed by the human mind and by how far we can expand ourselves."

This event served up many of channeling's main ingredients: eclecticism, an improvisational atmosphere, preoccupation with the future of humankind, and an emphasis on self-expansion. Although Paul's involvement with his guide seemed more focused on technology and less on spirituality than is typical of channels, the story of his initial meeting with Kana resembled many first-contact narratives. He reported an unexpected connection to a mysterious source, a return to ordinary wakefulness, and reassurance by witnesses that remarkable wisdom had poured forth during his trance. After an initial period of slow, awkward communication, Paul's link to Kana eventually became both easier to achieve and less taxing to sustain. Now, he said, the connection is an everyday part of his life. Although the people who attend Paul's channeling sessions experience this link only vicariously, Janet's comments imply that regular exposure to the drama of Paul's channeling confirms their sense of the vastness of human potential.

The validity of experiences such as this is questioned by skeptics who consider channeling a form of self-delusion or, worse still, a pathetic hoax. Nevertheless, at least one scientific study has shown that channeling produces a distinctive brainwave signature, suggesting that channels achieve a specific altered state of consciousness.[1] Paul's trance-like state and his inability to recall most of what happens during the channeling session are classic features of what psychologists call dissociation, a mental state marked by divided consciousness or "at least momentarily unbridgeable compartmentalization of experiences."[2] Dissociative experiences range in intensity from casual daydreaming to the complete loss of personal identity. In many cultures, people actively seek dissociative states through sleep deprivation, fasting, drumming, frenetic dancing, or the use of hallucinogenic drugs, often as part of their religious practices. The quest for altered states of consciousness is so widely found in human societies that it may reflect a deep-seated biological need still only dimly understood by science.

Euro-American culture is unusual in its unwillingness to grant dissociation an honored place in human experience. Although psychologists make half-hearted allowance for occasional dream-like states or out-of-body experiences, they are inclined to consider dissociation an expression of mental illness, and their categories of dissociative disorders continue to proliferate accordingly. The most highly publicized dissociative condition is multiple personality, recently reclassified as Dissociative Identity Disorder. The reality of multiple personality is still contested among mental health professionals, but it has earned a place in the diagnostic manual of the American Psychiatric Association (usually referred to as the *DSM-IV*), which defines it as "the presence of two or more distinct identities or personality states that recurrently take control of behavior."[3]

The histories of multiple personality and channeling are linked in curious ways. Many of psychiatry's early figures, both in Europe and the United States, were fascinated by spiritualism, a precursor to channeling. Sigmund Freud belonged to the Society for Psychical Research for a time, although he later came to regard mediumship as a form of neurosis. Despite Freud's move away from spiritualism, he retained the idea that the self was fundamentally multiple, with ego, id, and superego carrying on a ceaseless internal quarrel. Like their European counterparts, American psychiatrists eventually distanced themselves from spiritualism but not from the characteristically American fascination with self-expansion, which reemerged in their willingness to accept multiple personality as a real condition. Later I shall assess the ways in which multiple personality and channeling are again converging in contemporary psychotherapy. For the moment, however, let it suffice to say that the two are separated by a critical difference: multiple personality is experienced as a mental disturbance that produces acute dysfunction, whereas channeling is, with few exceptions, a process that its practitioners find beneficial. When a researcher administered identical psychological tests to channels and to people diagnosed with multiple personality, she found that the two populations in fact had little in common.[4]

When compared to other altered states of consciousness, chan-

neling has two key features. First, it involves a mild form of dissociation that usually begins after only a few minutes of meditation.
Once in the appropriate state of mind, channels adopt a distinctive speaking style and body language.[5] Second, channeling in-
duces an emotional state that practitioners experience as a distinct
personality or consciousness. The language used to talk about this
other personality, however, varies greatly, even in the statements
of a single person. A Connecticut woman who channels a being
named Amos, for instance, refused to refer to him as an entity, a
term widely used among channels. "I don't like the word entity
because it makes Amos seem like a thing. Amos is multiple energies. His energy is a composite of Michael and the Archangel Gabriel." She explained that when channeling this energy she is
"connecting with the higher self, what Jung called the collective
unconscious." For her, these different formulations—"being,"
"energy," "higher self," "collective unconscious"—were in no
way incompatible.

Channels show different degrees of commitment to the sep-
arateness of their entities or spirit guides. Some are deeply involved in the biographies and personality traits of the entities,
whether they are angels or warriors from Atlantis. Belief in the
individuality of spirit guides reaches its zenith among the small
but apparently growing number of channels who identify themselves as "walk-ins," that is, people whose bodies have been
taken over by extraterrestrials. Walk-ins, who refer to the physical body as their "ground crew" and take names straight from
science-fiction novels (Kadar Mon-Ka or Jalendra or ZrenDar),
claim to represent organizations like the Intergalactic Council
of Light or the Mother Ship Starbase, which use sophisticated
technologies to intervene in human affairs. A case could be
made that walk-ins are not channels in the strict sense, since

they have given up the identity that was their original reference point and taken on a new one. In practice, most walk-ins continue to channel what they describe as energies from their home base, wherever it is located.

Channels explain that spirits, energies, or alien forms of consciousness contact humans for many reasons. Some want to push humanity along the path of spiritual perfection. Others confess more self-interested motives, including a desire to improve the planet before they reincarnate in human form. Some are simply curious about life on our plane of existence. Without exception, channels describe these beings as having benevolent intentions. Demons or negative energies, channels insist, are too disorganized to manifest themselves in humans who make a conscious effort to channel only positive spirits or, as they are often called, "beings of light." Still, even encounters with helpful, caring spirits are not without risks. In his exhaustive study of channeling, the transpersonal psychologist Arthur Hastings warns without a trace of irony that channels should be careful not to enter into codependent relationships with their spirit guides, since this can lead to emotional abuse. Hastings recommends that there be "negotiation between the entity and the person to respect the needs of each."[6]

Spirits share knowledge that reflects their prior experience and current vantage point. The wisest spirits have undergone many incarnations and thus graduated to a different plane or dimension. From their outpost beyond earthly notions of space and time, they can see possible futures, hence their value as a source of predictions. The recently dead, in contrast, may offer some useful information, but they are still too close to the passions and fears of earthly life to be completely objective. Channels are not above occasional boasting about the relative superiority of their sources. In Santa Fe, a channel named Jill Parsons recommended avoiding second-rate spirits. "If you're going to get information, you have to go to the highest sources," she said. "You don't want to channel the astral plane," she continued, referring to the second level of a seven-level hierarchy based on the teachings of the Theosophical Society, "because that's like hanging out at Bud's Bar and Grill." Jill and other channels who believe in ranked levels of spiritual understanding are likely to describe their guides as Ascended Masters or members of the Great White Brotherhood, references to beings whose gilt-edged credentials were established a century ago by Helena Petrovna Blavatsky (1831–1891), the Russian mystic and spiritualist who in 1875 co-founded the Theosophical Society, an organization whose occult teachings have strongly influenced the contemporary New Age movement.[7]

This obsession with celestial rank has its critics. One outspoken Santa Fe channel lampooned the Great White Brotherhood as "male hierarchical garbage." "I make a joke with my clients," he said. "I say that if some people channel the Ascended Masters, then I channel the Descended Mistresses." A man involved in metaphysical work in New England astringently referred to the Ascended Masters as "British colonialism on the spiritual plane." A compromise position voiced by some channels is that the location from which an entity speaks affects the kind but not the quality of information conveyed, thus implying that even the wisest spirits have limits. Those who never occupied a physical body, for instance, cannot offer useful advice on human health. Spirits from the distant past cannot be counted on for insight into the stock market. (As one channel wryly put it, "I found out that none of my spirit guides knows about bankruptcy laws in California.") Beings from one plane might provide messages that focus on issues regarding emotions, whereas those coming from another may be more philosophical. Whatever the source of a spirit's wisdom, its mission is to offer a fresh view of human life. Adam, a channel from New Mexico, framed it this way: "An entity gives people a different viewpoint. Entities are truly interested in growth. They help people find a state where they can access their own information, become their own channel, connect to their own Christ-self."

Adam's comment is typical of channeling's humanist wing, which rejects a focus on powerful aliens or spiritual masters on the grounds that it promotes separation of the human from the divine. Adam and other humanist channels insist that channeling provides an upward link to our higher self, an eternal and transcendent core that knows the answers to all of life's questions. A broader concept than the conventional idea of soul, the higher self represents our unique, personal fragment of the universal whole. Channels committed to this vision insist that the names and features of their sources are artificial constructs that give a human face to powers beyond our comprehension.

Beliefs about spiritual sources thus wheel around opposing themes. Channels and their clients see the self as vast, eternal, and protean, taking on new shapes as it evolves. As one channel put it, we are "multidimensional beings living simultaneously on all dimensions back to God-All-That-Is." In that sense, we share in God's oneness. But if the idea of oneness is pushed too far, the self would dissolve into the totality of everything. That might be acceptable to Buddhists, but it is unappealing to Americans convinced that each of us is unique in the universe. The distinctive personalities of spirit guides can be seen as proof that however malleable the self, some essential core lives for-ever, whether as Ascended Masters in another dimension or as homespun souls on the astral plane.

Channels vigorously disagree about what happens to their everyday self while they are channeling, an ambiguity that has produced a major split between advocates of trance channeling and those who prefer conscious channeling.[8] Trance channels, of whom J. Z. Knight is a prominent example, claim to experi-ence a complete separation of their selves from the spirits they channel. Their bodies become empty vessels for spiritual intel-ligence. Trance channels remember little of what happens when they are in an altered state, although they differ in their assess-ment of how "absent" they are during channeling sessions. Some argue that the conscious self must step aside completely for the channeling to work. Others contend that the conscious self merely moves over to make enough space for the spirits to squeeze in. Bryan Wood, who regularly channels a collective spirit called The Clan in deep trances, said, "When describing my trance, I tell people that it's as though I'm immersed in water and The Clan is the water in which I'm immersed. We join in a cooperative venture."

Unlike trance channels, conscious channels remain aware of what happens around them while they communicate with spir-its. "When I channel," one man explained, "it's like being at a party and overhearing another conversation. At the same time, the entity uses my mind, my vernacular, perhaps my memory." For conscious channels, spirits are allies, not replacements for the ordinary self. The full implications of the contrast between trance and conscious channeling can be seen by examining the performances of exemplary practitioners of each.

In June 1993 the Omega Institute in Rhinebeck, New York, offered a workshop by Kevin Ryerson, a nationally-known trance channel who serves as a medium for several colorful spirits.[9] Omega, one of the largest of the many personal-growth centers now springing up throughout the United States, has been described as a "spiritual summer camp for adults."[10] In fact, its sleek administration building looks less like a camp than a Hilton on the first night of a professional convention, even if the prevailing dress code calls for natural-fiber clothing and sandals. The institute's grounds, which include a Japanese meditation garden and scattered works of sculpture, succeed in fostering a contemplative mood.

On a warm Saturday morning Kevin Ryerson greeted the workshop participants, approximately forty people ranging in age from 19 to the mid-sixties. Ryerson, a large man with a ponytail, looked more like a retired linebacker than a guru. But despite his informal and occasionally self-deprecating manner, he proved to be articulate, well-organized, and lively. Ryerson acknowledged the links between his own gift and those of nineteenth- and early-twentieth-century spiritualists, a historical connection recognized by few other channels. In his opening remarks he disarmed potential skeptics by acknowledging that channeling can be seen as a poetic or metaphorical process rather than a literal one, although he harbors no personal doubts about its empirical reality. His bulk sprawled in a chair, Ryerson told the group that channeling is directly linked to forms of shamanism practiced in "ancient, holistic cultures." Like shamanism, Ryerson said, channeling rejects analytical and critical thought, which he dismissed as "safety blankets" that prevent us from direct knowing on the emotional and intuitive levels. "Our society is devoid of healing psychic imagery, so we allow ourselves to be overwhelmed by technology," he said. "We have a heroic course: to step out of our world into the sacred wheel of this building, a sacred mandala, and enter a new paradigm to find out who we are."

When asked how he could tap into spiritual beings on demand, Ryerson likened the spirit world to a vast library. "Intelligences from other places and times are available in books. Using these books, we can draw from those times and cultures. Channels are trained to tap into these intelligences directly. They establish trust and rapport with other intelligences. With much work, this contact becomes regular and comfortable." Ryerson described his own state when channeling as a form of "benign amnesia," since he recovers the experience only by listening to recordings made during his trance. The strong personalities of the beings that he channels leave him no doubt that he has contacted separate intelligences rather than his own higher self. As the workshop continued through the morning, Ryerson outlined his concepts on a flip chart, turning the workshop into a New Age chalk-talk reminiscent of a college physics class.

After lunch, Ryerson cheerfully announced that it was time for us to meet his entities. As if headed for home, Ryerson said goodbye. He rubbed his face, closed his eyes, and folded his hands in his lap. His head fell back, and he sighed with a deep rasping sound. Thirty seconds later, he began to speak in a hoarse whisper, the voice of an entity called John the Essene, who lived in biblical times. The voice asked for the subject of the day's talk. Ryerson's wife, who assisted him during the workshop, explained where the group was and what it wished to discuss.

John carried on in a gruff whisper: "It has been said that time is like a river that flows as though both into the past and into the future. Verily, verily I say unto thee, time is more so like a pool, out of which you may pull up past, present, future, or state of being at any moment."

The stilted phrasing and nearly inaudible voice were hard to follow, and some people began to squirm restlessly in the mounting afternoon heat. Then the flow of John's monologue halted abruptly. Ryerson's voice changed to the melodious stage-Irish lilt of Tom MacPherson, sixteenth-century pick-pocket: "MacPherson here. And how are the lot of you doing out there?" "Fine," several members of the audience replied. "It is quite a large room, is it not? 'Tis a bit round, not unlike as though the Globe of me own day. That is, the Globe being the stage, so to say. Now, if you will, each of you are performers upon the stage. All's you need to do is to reach deep into the passions, if you will, and all that you need then is to have your ears open to the thunderous applause of an appreciative audience." After additional comments in this vein, MacPherson bid farewell with a cheerful, "May the saints be lookin' after you."

No sooner had the spirit of the effusive Irishman departed than the group was greeted by a deeper voice. This urbane baritone proved to be Atun-Re, a Nubian priest and advisor to Akhenaton who lived around 1300 B.C., although the languid accent was reminiscent of Charles Aznavour. Atun-Re alternately charmed and badgered the audience, repeatedly asking, "Do you understand? Do you follow? Isn't that interesting?" If the group failed to respond with sufficient vigor, he became testy: "You humans haven't evolved much in three thousand years, have you?"

By now, everyone was used to the shifting cast of characters. All basked in the irreverent humor of Tom MacPherson and

Atun-Re, even laughing at Atun-Re's terrible jokes. At one point he joyfully plagiarized the punchline of a popular country-western song by referring to Cleopatra as the "Queen of Denial." When someone tried to help him as he struggled to find a word, he barked out, "I may be three thousand years old, but I'm not senile!" Eventually the group settled into more serious discussion. Women in the front row peppered him with questions. "Did you use crystals for healing in ancient Egypt?" "Tell us about the medical advances we can expect in the next twenty years." "Do you see an increase in terrorism in the world?" "Will we solve the energy crisis?"

By late afternoon, Kevin Ryerson was tiring. Atun-Re said goodbye as Ryerson covered his face with his hands. The voice of John the Essene reemerged, intoning a brief closing prayer. Moments later, Ryerson opened his eyes. During the entire process, he had remained seated, his body movements largely confined to hand gestures. He genially fielded a few questions from the group. When someone asked him why Atun-Re speaks English rather than Nubian, he explained that "Spirit must use the neuromotor responses that I'm conditioned with."

The second day of the workshop was a mixture of informal lecture, discussion, and channeling. For all of Kevin Ryerson's arguments against analytical thought, he and Atun-Re managed to lay out a schematic vision linking past lives, chakras (the body's energy centers), the architecture of Frank Lloyd Wright, crop circles, intuition, and ecology. Sometimes, however, the farrago of ideas veered out of control. In one breathless passage, Atun-Re articulated his vision of the future: "The electronic town meeting will become a voting booth. There will be popular voting from an enlightened perspective, based on a global identity. The fundamentalisms will subside. Moods and emotions will be stimulated and healed through color. Architecture will become seamless with the environment. Dependence on nuclear and fossil fuels will be obsolete. Diet will become the principal source of health, and there will be a planetary aquaculture based on Maya, Inca, and Aztec traditions."

As the day wore on, it became evident that there was a subtle tension between members of the group who, fascinated by the drama of channeling, wanted Ryerson to do more, and Ryerson himself, who seemed more interested in the content of the messages than in the exotic means of their production. He tried gamely, and largely successfully, to balance the two competing interests. As the famous channel closed up shop, autograph seekers crowded around with copies of his latest book, which was selling briskly at Omega's bookstore.

Ryerson expressed the view that channeling represents a new form of global shamanism, in the interests of which he is a popularizer. His work, he explained, "is a tool to help people make transitions in their lives." In his comments to the group, he casually referred to channeling's "entertainment quality," thereby implying that the theatrical nature of his performances was in part a way to expose a large audience to important metaphysical understandings. At the same time, he missed no opportunity to convince his audience of the historical reality of the flamboyant personalities that he channels. Ryerson mentioned, for instance, that the spirit of John the Essene had revealed to him the exact location of a buried city in the Holy Land, the existence of which was subsequently confirmed by an archaeological excavation.

The histrionics of Kevin Ryerson and other trance channels are regarded as problematic by some outspoken conscious channels, however. Marianne Rose, a California woman and a practitioner of conscious channeling, dismissed the drama of deep trance as "a parlor trick." "Trance channeling," she explained, "is basically done for drama's sake in order to prove to people that you're channeling—as if changing your voice actually did something." Along with other practitioners of conscious channeling, Marianne Rose sees deep trance as a useful but temporary step toward the integration of spiritual guidance into everyday life. Trance channeling, in other words, is something that people outgrow.[11] Several channels reported, in fact, that they gradually moved from trance channeling to conscious channeling as their understanding matured. This was consistent with what they saw as their growing intimacy with spirit guides. Only one claimed the opposite trajectory. A Santa Fe channel who began his career as a conscious channel reported that an awareness of his entity's words led him to feel too responsible for the information, especially if the news upset his clients. His emotional reaction caused the flood of information to "back up," giving him various physical ailments that healed only when he abandoned conscious channeling and began to channel from a deep trance.

Skeptics find the linguistic quirks of channels such as Kevin Ryerson to be irresistible targets for their debunking efforts. A linguist who studied the performances of several channels found that when they claim to be speaking in the voice of someone from another epoch, their speech is larded with anachronistic words or expressions.[12] A more obvious problem is an inconsistent vocabulary. At one moment a spirit may struggle to find a common English word, as if to show unfamiliarity with the language ("that place of the dead that you call—is it a cemetery?"), and the next it will drop an obscure colloquialism, usually for comic effect ("Tell me the truth; I'll know if you're fibbing.").

Channels rationalize these idiosyncrasies by pointing out that spirits depend on the neurological structure of their human host, which explains why they don't speak in foreign languages and, when they communicate in English, why their accents tend to wander. Anyway, they argue, the point of channeling is to jog people out of their complacency and propel them toward higher consciousness, so the stranger the speaking style the better. They make a valid point. Religious ceremonies throughout the world use unusual vocabularies, even entire ritual languages, to separate sacred space and time from everyday life. The enduring popularity of the Latin Mass among some Roman Catholics, which has withstood the Church's efforts to eradicate it, reminds us that unconventional language is not as distant from American rituals as we might suppose.[13]

In sharp contrast to the drama of trance channeling is the form of conscious channeling practiced by David and Sasha Johnson, a husband and wife team who regularly give workshops in major cities on both coasts. Sasha's Scandinavian features contrast with David's darker hair and complexion, but together they make a handsome couple, and they seem genuinely at ease with one another despite obvious differences in temperament. By their own appraisal, Sasha is intuitive and emotion-oriented, whereas David, who holds a doctorate in counseling, is more analytical. These complementary qualities serve as bricks and mortar for their joint lectures, which address issues of the day and personal questions posed by members of the audience. So low-keyed is their connection to the spirit world that one wouldn't know that they were channeling if they hadn't announced in advance that they would be connecting to an entity named Michael.

At their public talks, David and Sasha usually explain that Michael is a collective of many beings rather than an individual spirit. The name assigned to the group reflects the human need to personalize a more abstract concept. The Michael Teachings, as they are sometimes called, are as close to a channeling franchise as one can find in the United States today. Channeled by several psychics in the Bay Area in the early 1970s, Michael is said to be the source of a complex body of spiritual and psychological information central to the work of perhaps three dozen professional channels, mostly on the West Coast, and an unknown number of others whose links to Michael are more sporadic. Based on the concept of progressive reincarnations, the Michael Teachings offer a formal system of personality categories that help to explain the needs and proclivities of people as they live out each of the lifetimes on their path toward spiritual maturity. The Michael Educational Foundation, in Orinda, California, serves as the central clearinghouse for the teachings that have developed around this collectively channeled spirit entity.[14]

David and Sasha Johnson were raised in southern California but moved to the Bay Area as young adults. In the 1960s David experimented with psychedelics, enrolled in Erhard Seminars Training *(est),* and journeyed to India and Thailand. After receiving his bachelor's degree, he studied at a well-known psychotherapeutic institute in Berkeley, which he described as "very traditional, very staid." Sasha's career interests were in business, and while David trained as a psychotherapist she managed a large real estate office.

In the late 1970s they joined a Bay Area group that was quietly developing its links to the entities called Michael. To his surprise, David found that connecting to Michael helped his psychotherapy practice by giving him a better intuitive sense of the emotional needs of clients. He soon grew more confident in his ability to identify their problems quickly by using his gut rather than his brain. Sasha, who worked as a real estate agent, had similar experiences in a totally different context: "For me, it wasn't ever a thing like, 'Now I'm going to channel,' with a big bolt of lightning. It was a subtle changeover. I started using the channeled information when I took the job as office manager. I had twenty-five or thirty agents working for me, and everyone would come to me with their problems. I started receiving channeled information that improved my management skills. It was amazing how that office became very successful and everyone got along. I became known for my skill at solving problems and serving as an arbitrator. Looking back, I realize that a lot of it hinged on my ability to get information from Michael."

Sasha and David described the process of communicating with Michael as subtle rather than dramatic. Sasha connects to the "Michael energy" more or less at will, while David needs a more formal process to activate his link. "I usually do a specific meditation to bring myself into channeling," he explained. "I'm intellectually centered, so I need something to move me out of that." He described the transition as a movement from the intellect to a deeper, more intuitive kind of knowing. Watching David and Sasha give channeled lectures, their connection to Michael is perceptible only as a slight pause in their speech and more reflective answers to questions posed by an audience. Throughout the process they are completely alert.

Unlike the careers of trance channels such as Kevin Ryerson, which tend to emphasize dramatic performance, the conscious channeling technique perfected by David and Sasha Johnson lends itself to conventional counseling and workshops in personal development. Their story emphasizes practicality and control rather than a sudden personal transformation. David and Sasha advertise channeled counseling services at $110 an hour, a rate comparable to orthodox psychotherapy, and by all appearances they have prospered. David recently appeared on a nationally broadcast television talk show, discussing his new book about techniques for recognizing the strengths and weaknesses of one's personality traits.

From the perspective of trance channels, conscious channeling like that practiced by the Johnsons is flawed because a listener cannot easily separate the message from the messenger. The information provided by conscious channels, they argue, may be "contaminated by ego"—in other words, too strongly influenced by the consciousness of the channel. Trance channels, in contrast, are effectively absent during their channeling sessions, offering their clients direct, unmediated contact with spiritual entities.

Discussion between advocates of trance channeling and those who favor conscious channeling lurches between a set of conflicting ideals. Trance channels try to push aside the ego, making room for pure knowledge from a higher source. But their denial of the self violates an equally important principle of New Age thought, the self's fundamental greatness. When they suspend personal consciousness by offering their body to a spirit entity, trance channels have implicitly admitted that the spirit is higher, better, more powerful—qualities that conflict with the notion that humans are themselves capable of infinite wisdom. A woman passionately committed to conscious channeling argued that the trance-channeling model is no longer useful. "To me that's an old understanding," she said. "Trance channels are saying that you're the poor peon who has to make the connection and put yourself aside so that something wonderful will happen. But now we're in a completely different cycle, and we're here to honor ourselves." Yet even conscious channels feel compelled to define themselves as "clear," meaning that they bring in metaphysical knowledge untainted by personal motives. The reverse side of this debate is the question of whether the channel opens to inner or outer space—that is, a more celestial part of the self or an autonomous being utterly different from the self. As one might expect, trance channels are more likely to argue for the latter. Virtually all channels agree, however, that at some level of abstraction it does not matter whether the channeled consciousness is self or other. The act of channeling itself proves that humans have untapped powers which, if acknowledged and refined, can connect us to other dimensions and universes, thereby expanding the self far beyond its present limits.

Although trance channels and conscious channels profess different approaches to spirit communication, their performances actually fall along a continuum. Kevin Ryerson and the Johnsons represent two extremes. Most channels operate closer to the spectrum's middle, where performances of trance and conscious channeling are hard to distinguish. In this middle ground, the major difference between trance and conscious channeling is that the former are more immobilized by trance and less likely to recall the words of their spirit contacts. Since 1990 there seems to have been a significant shift in popularity in the direction of conscious channeling. Channels generally confirmed this, observing that the change reflects the integration of spirituality into daily life. Martha, a conscious channel from Santa Fe, described the pleasures of omnipresent spirit guides: "For me it's like always having friends around. When I need to, I can just fall back into their energy. It's like collapsing into a big comfy chair." The routinization of channeling described by Martha makes sense in practical terms as well. Because trance channels experience nearly complete disorientation, they usually need help during their channeling sessions: someone to operate a tape recorder, handle situations that arise in the room, and so on. This presents few problems during large public performances, but it does not lend itself to the private sessions and telephone work that put bread on the table of professional channels. Conscious channels find their style more compatible with the starts and stops of private counseling.

The common goal of all channels is to *link up,* to make an emotionally satisfying connection to higher powers and to their own divine essence. The actual form that this connection takes, however, reflects characteristically American dilemmas about the self—whether, for instance, it should submit to some authoritative master plan at the expense of personal autonomy or instead blaze its own lonely trail. Most channels succeed in having it both ways by appropriating the language of higher authority and using it to exalt the self, a strategy illustrated in a channeling publication which assures readers that spirit guides will use their wisdom "to encourage you to find your own solutions to problems and . . . not to give your power away to them by doing something simply because they have suggested it."[15] If the spirit guides often sound like cosmic psychotherapists, laughing at human foibles but rarely offering reproach or criticism, it is because channels and their clients take the therapeutic ethos that so thoroughly permeates our age and project it onto the limitless screen of the universe.

3

CHANNELED THEOLOGY

Jon Lockwood, a channel from northern New Mexico, met me late in 1993 in the comfortable living room of his friend and collaborator Janice Chenaille. Both are interior designers, and Janice's talent was on display in the apartment. The room's high ceilings were crossed by huge *vigas,* the rough-hewn logs that these days serve less as structural features than as emblems of Santa Fe Style. A fire crackled in a corner hearth, helping to illuminate several fine Navajo rugs and pieces of Southwestern furniture. Jon, a handsome man in his thirties, sat near the fire. His long blonde hair was set off by black jeans, a turtleneck, and cowboy boots. Janice, elegantly dressed in a dark sweater and charcoal slacks, sat across a coffee-table from Jon. In her late forties, she described herself as a former corporate wife from the Deep South. Divorce and a search for spiritual fulfillment had recently brought her to New Mexico.

Jon was raised in a small hill town in Maryland. Two themes dominated his turbulent childhood: the mental illness of his father, a condition that eventually shattered his parents' marriage, and Jon's grow-

ing awareness of his own homosexuality, which led him to contemplate suicide during his teens. At first he sought solace in his
local Methodist congregation, later in psychedelics and mari-
juana. After high school, he discovered that he had a talent for
art that earned him a scholarship at a design school in Los Angeles. Degree in hand, Jon moved to New Mexico with his
longtime partner, a man whom he met in Maryland around the
time he revealed to his family that he was gay.

Jon explained that prior to 1986 his exposure to channeling
and related spiritual practices was minimal. But from the moment he sat down to read one of Shirley MacLaine's books, parts
of which describe her experiences with several famous channels,
he was "overcome with waves of energy." He began to attend a
weekly class taught by a local channel whose goal was to teach
others to contact their spirit guides. "The first night of the class,"
Jon said, "I was told by the teacher's entity that my purpose was
to be an antenna"—that is, to receive channeled messages. Despite initial skepticism, Jon was soon channeling on his own.
After a period of experimentation, he established a link with
Ariel, a being with whom he instantly felt a strong affinity. Jon
described Ariel as a "seventh-dimensional energy" that originates in a distant galaxy.

For a time, Jon channeled regularly for large groups, but he
found that this pushed his physical resources to the limit. He suffered from chronic headaches and fatigue. Worse still, the people for whom he channeled failed to respect his privacy. They
called late at night or early in the morning for channeled information that would solve their urgent personal problems. Eventually he had to set boundaries. He began to limit his public
channeling to small groups of friends, only occasionally working
with larger groups. He and Janice began to work as a team after

they made a pilgrimage to Sedona, Arizona, a place revered in the channeling community for its potent "vortex" sites, locations said to concentrate cosmic energies. During a meditation at Airport Mesa, Sedona's best-known sacred site, Jon's entity Ariel went into Janice's body and activated her own spiritual potential, an experience that she said instantly made her aware of the universe's unconditional love. Now Janice usually attends Jon's channeling sessions, where she assists him by "grounding his energy"—that is, helping him to maintain a sense of physical balance and well-being—and occasionally administering hands-on healing to Jon's clients.

One evening I joined Jon, Janice, and various friends who had gathered to converse with Ariel. As Jon settled into a lotus position on the couch, Janice tied back his hair to prevent it from flying into his face when Ariel took over. Jon closed his eyes. His head dropped for several minutes. His body began to shake, and he emitted a series of low grunts. Ariel emerged as a high-energy voice speaking with an accent that was at times vaguely British, then colloquially American. As he channeled, Jon looked like a blonde Buddha on amphetamines. He laughed with gusto and gestured expressively with his hands: "Hello, my friends. I'm very excited to be in the body again. So! It's interesting what's happening on your planet in these times, yes? And who's got the key? Who's the one who's got the right to touch divinity? Each and every one of *you,* my friends! All the universe is applauding! Look at them touching their divinity!"

Emerging from his trance an hour later, Jon summarized Ariel's message this way: "Ariel doesn't predict doom and gloom. He applauds us. He honors the human race for its evolution. Ariel says that this is the end of His-story, and that before that was Her-story, and that we're evolving toward God's-story. Listening to him, you almost can't wait until it happens."

When we spoke eighteen months later, Jon reported that after several years of struggling to bring the physical demands of his channeling gift into some kind of balance, he was now in "alignment" with the energy of Ariel. This hard-won equilibrium allowed him to channel more frequently, thus taking Ariel's message to a wider audience. Jon was now conducting individual counseling with clients in New Mexico and California and occasionally offering group sessions. He mentioned that during one recent period Ariel went on strike, insisting that Janice and other members of Jon's informal study group begin to channel for themselves. Even more dramatic was the appearance of Jesus in their midst—or at least a "Jesus energy" that each of them channeled during a few memorable evenings. "What's happening now," Jon said, "is the second coming of Christ. That's when Christ appears inside each of us." Jon's interpretation was that the spiritual energy of Christ was returning to repair the damage caused by conventional Christian churches. Like the life stories of many channels, Jon's is organized around a millenarian theme. He believes that his own life, and that of the wider society, is headed toward spiritual fulfillment that will transform the world, a view expressed on a New Age bumpersticker that proclaims, "Shift happens."

Jon's creative enthusiasm conjures up an image of the eccentric American inventor tinkering in his basement. Dissatisfied with institutional religion, Jon, Janice, and their friends are appropriating Christianity to meet their personal needs—in this case by each becoming Christ, at least for the period of their highly-charged channeling sessions. Such improvisation is the engine that drives contemporary channeling, which as much as

anything is characterized by a kaleidoscopic reordering of traditional themes to suit the preoccupations of the moment. Jon
framed his quest in a key American idiom when he described
channeling as a way of "redefining who we are." "The channeling process," he insisted, "is about sovereignty."

As Jon's comments imply, the sovereignty sought by most
channels makes them wary of religious orthodoxy of any kind.
Although a few channels have authored best-selling works that
are considered authoritative in some respects, even admirers are
careful to stipulate that no single message is appropriate for
everyone. At the heart of this reluctance to accept any truth as
universally valid is a rejection of habits of mind based on analytical reason.

Analytical reason, channels are fond of saying, is a legitimate
way of knowing, but it has come to dominate our civilization
in destructive ways. To counteract the tyranny of rationality,
they advocate a turn toward the emotions and the body as a way
of fostering more balanced human development. Channels constantly tell their clients, "Feel things in your body" or "Let your
body share its knowing." Attainment of this holism requires the
suspension of "judgment," a term that for them carries only
negative connotations. "Judgment means that we are more
aware than someone else, which creates separation," a Santa Fe
channel explained. In other words, believing that one answer is
better than another cuts us off from those who hold different
views, and it limits our ability to make use of those alternative
views in the future, thus reducing personal options. Judgments
about truth and error also fan the flames of sectarian struggle,
setting people against one another in endless arguments over orthodoxy and heresy.

If analytical judgments are inherently negative, how does one measure the accuracy of channeled information? Linda Butler, a Massachusetts woman who values channeled teachings, explained that to separate good information from bad she "listens to the channels' tone of voice and feels their energy." Then she asks her own spirit guides, "Is this for real?" People are advised to accept channeled information only if it works for *them*—that is, if it is personally meaningful and clarifies key events in their lives. According to Sally Roberts, a woman from New Mexico, "Channeled information obtained in a private session should be an affirmation of who you perceive yourself to be." From this perspective, spiritual insight can be accepted or rejected according to the dictates of personal intuition. In Santa Fe, the channel Bryan Wood emphasized, "No information source can abrogate a person's free will."

During long workshops and extended interviews, this reluctance to judge occasionally fell away in the face of truly outlandish claims. Instead of blunt criticism, judgment took the form of sly shrugs or ironic comments on the order of "To each his own." Sometimes people gently mocked the excesses of famous channels or the pompous utterances of local gurus. A parody flier that circulated in Santa Fe in the early 1990s announced a workshop to help people "lower their self-esteem naturally," warning that "healing the child within may involve costly dental work." Another advertised the services of a clever spirit named Gerry, once a financial adviser to the Pharaohs and now an expert on Santa Fe real estate. The flier included a testimonial from a satisfied client who gushed, "Gerry is the only entity who stays with you right up to the title search."[1]

Despite occasional lapses of neutrality, however, the consensus among channels and their clients is that truth is ultimately personal and situational. When channeled predictions of natu-

ral disaster prove to be false, for example, the error is rational-
ized by speculating that those who believed the warning actually benefitted by being jarred out of their complacency. As one
woman said about prophecies of doom, "I'm not into the fear
mode myself, but it's another perspective. Some people need to
go through fear modes in order to come up out of them." False
predictions, in other words, contain their own kind of truth.

If truth is personal, then channeling not only accommodates
contradictory visions but actually needs that variety to meet the
demands of people who are themselves infinitely diverse. Their
personal truths will vary according to where they are on the
path of self-discovery. Later, they can discard one set of beliefs
in favor of another more appropriate to their circumstances. A
contributor to an Internet discussion forum likened channeled
messages to television programs. "Do you complain about the
conflicting messages you get from different programs on TV?
Probably what you do is decide which one you're most comfortable with and watch it regularly." Sandy Randolph, a New
Mexico channel, noted that disappointment about a false prophecy of doom proved to be a major turning point in her life,
showing her that channeled information, whatever its source,
had to be tested against inner knowing. Almost any declaration
will be true for someone, so there are few grounds for labeling
assertions as nonsense.

This laissez-faire attitude toward truth leads to the prolifera-
tion of improbable claims of angelic manifestations, dimensional
shifts, hovering spaceships, and imminent natural disasters in the
numerous small-circulation magazines that cater to the channeling community. A reader dipping into an issue of one of the
glossiest of these magazines would find, among other things, a
map of North America as it is expected to appear after un-

specified, but clearly dramatic, natural disasters that will erase the states of Maine, Louisiana, California, Oregon, and Washington.[2] Information that circulates on the Internet is even more questionable. One on-line journal advertised a "Reverse Channeling Facilitator" that allows users to "channel out of your body and project into the bodies of other life forms throughout the universe." Priced at $44, it includes a headband lined with meteorites, minerals, and crystals.[3]

Faced with such dubious claims and prophecies, those who fret about the state of American education have warned of an alarming increase in public irrationality. In the vanguard of this campaign is CSICOP, the Committee for the Scientific Investigation of Claims of the Paranormal, an organization whose journal, the *Skeptical Inquirer,* attempts to debunk everything from UFOs to astrology. The missionary zeal of CSICOP's activities is driven by fear that our nation faces an "apocalypse of unreason," a new Dark Age in which growing irrationality will prevent us from solving the urgent problems of our time.[4]

Although it is doubtful that Americans are much more irrational today than in the past, the alarmists of CSICOP may be right when they observe a significant shift in truth standards among the nation's educated classes. For the past two decades, scientific habits of mind have come under withering criticism from academic humanists, who accuse the natural sciences of purveying in their institutions and methods a "politics of male supremacy, class exploitation, racism, and imperialism," to quote the indictment of one prominent scholar.[5] The arguments advanced by the critics of science are complex, but they coalesce around several themes. One is that by its very nature Western science is male-centered and therefore dominated by masculine notions of power. Another is that science is inherently biased against perspectives that come from outside the cultural mainstream. Like many sophisticated arguments, the academic critique of science percolates into mass culture stripped of its original subtlety.

Those involved in channeling often have a general familiarity with academic attacks on science even if they show little interest in their details. The argument that Western science is ethnocentric, however, is appealing to an audience that believes in the redemptive power of ancient, pre-scientific knowledge, especially as preserved by American Indians and other native peoples. Many, in fact, believe that only this knowledge will save humanity from self-destruction.

Other social forces help to create a climate in which highly relativistic notions of truth can prosper. Contemporary multicultural politics, for instance, leads routinely to claims that social identities create unique ways of understanding the world. Although the more radical manifestos of identity-based knowledge—Afrocentrism, for example—are still contested, the broader claim that facts are determined by the identity of the observer is now virtually undisputed in the public arena. Meanwhile, public-relations experts in the employ of corporate clients assert that truth is infinitely variable, a contest of stories or viewpoints rather than of facts.[6] They articulate a pervasive view of reality that now guides advertising, tabloid journalism, and political campaigns.

These social currents converge in the epistemological framework of channeling, where they are distilled into the guiding principle that all meaningful truth is personal. As one channel states in a document published on the Internet, the goal of spiritual exploration should be to "question, explore, doubt, and discover through your *own* channel what the truth really is."[7] "It may not be my reality," channels are fond of saying, "but if it's yours, that's OK with me." Yet even epistemological relativists must share some basic assumptions about the world. With patient probing, one can find enough common elements to piece together a moral and philosophical framework that qualifies as a theology in the most general sense.

The first and most important theological postulate of channeling is that human beings are in essence gods. Kevin Ryerson, for instance, states unambiguously: "We are God, and God is love. We are here to manifest our own God-realized nature."[8] Other channels assert human divinity more obliquely, declaring that we are "fragments of the God-Head" or "Christed beings" put on earth for a spiritual purpose. Both metaphors imply that humans share in the divinity that created the universe. The inherent divinity of human beings means that we are immortal, inherently good, and fully able to create our own reality.[9]

The existence of a divine essence within each of us does not mean that we are all fully developed beings. Channels and their clients generally believe that humans undergo successive reincarnations to acquire important learning experiences, an evolutionary process that may include lifetimes in other planetary systems or dimensions. But reincarnation raises a knotty problem. If we inevitably cycle through countless lives—male and female, affluent and impoverished, human and extraterrestrial—then who are we? Do we have a meaningful self, and if so, what is it? Few channels express concern about this, however. They seem comfortable with the assumption that there is an irreducible quality of the self that persists, say, through successive incarnations as a Babylonian magician, a Saxon peasant, a Buddhist monk, and a powerful healer from another dimension.[10]

Standing beside reincarnation in channeling's theology is the doctrine that we are responsible for creating our own reality. Thoughts shape reality, channels argue, and the impact of any thought is magnified when a critical mass of like-minded people share it. The mythic charter for this belief is the Hundredth Monkey story, which is told and retold in personal-growth workshops across the nation. The Hundredth Monkey story is a wildly distorted version of a primatologist's report published in the 1950s. Scientists noted that macaques could teach one another to wash food that had been left for them by the researchers. In the New Age version of the tale, when the hundredth monkey learned the technique, knowledge of it jumped spontaneously to monkeys on other islands. The story implies that a mass shift in consciousness can quickly spread new ideas through the world. Ideas then change reality in the most literal sense.[11]

The claim that we can create our own reality would seem to be contradicted by the parallel belief that behavior is strongly influenced by incidents in previous lifetimes. In the course of private channeled sessions, for example, channels often reveal to clients that their current problems are rooted in fears or unresolved conflicts originating in earlier incarnations. But most channels insist that the pernicious influence of past-life problems can be countered by changes in attitude once the client is made aware of the hidden forces that stand in the way of creating a new and better personal reality.

The transformative power of thought connects to another sacred postulate of channeling: the transcendent value of holism. The purpose of channeling—and by extension, other forms of New Age spirituality—is to bring together elements of life ripped apart by Western civilization: science and religion, body and soul, culture and nature, male and female, reason and intuition, thought and matter. Where one half of a dichotomy has overpowered the other, channeling tries to strengthen the weaker partner. Hence the emphasis on intuition rather than intellect in Kevin Ryerson's workshop. Those involved in channeling insist that embodiment—experiencing things in the body—is needed to cure the negative effects of the mind games that plague modern life.

The search for holism extends far beyond attempts to reunify mind and body. Channels and their clients see the universe as a single interconnected field. Just as the thought patterns of individuals can reshape the cosmos, so shifts in the cosmos affect individuals. The spirits who speak through channels warn listeners of impending "earth changes" that influence all of us, whether we realize it or not. Earth changes may be dramatic— floods, epidemics, and earthquakes—or subtle, such as shifts in "spiritual frequencies" that stimulate a desire for personal change.

Sacred places, many of which are identified as vortex sites, assist this process by drawing in useful spiritual energies from other parts of the universe. Channels in New Mexico cited the southwestern landscape, held to be rich in vortex sites, as the major reason why people there are experiencing intense spiritual growth. Jill Parsons explained that an energy vortex south of Santa Fe accounts for the city's role as a center for alternative spirituality. "The vortex has been a place of spiritual opening. The Indians used this area for ceremonies. There's an openness to other realities and other dimensions." Vortex sites in Sedona, Arizona, receive 5,000 visitors a month during the summer tourist season, an influx that now supports several tour companies that take pilgrims to the principal sacred sites in colorful jeeps.[12]

Channels in vortex-deprived parts of the country often dismiss special claims about the Southwest, which they feel are exaggerated. A Massachusetts man deeply involved in such work insisted that power spots are a human phenomenon rather than something intrinsic to a place. "When a group of people get together for a level of communication that is clear and like-minded and flowing," he said, "they create a kind of energy that, in a sense, *becomes* a power spot." A recent workshop in New Hampshire promised to teach participants to "awaken the energy circulation" in their own area. Where people cannot find energy vortexes, in other words, they can now make their own.

A surprising number of the theological principles that underlie channeling were first enunciated by spiritualists in the nineteenth century. American spiritualism emerged in the late 1840s and peaked in the period between 1850 and 1875. In its heyday, spiritualism may have been followed by more than a million people, almost five percent of the U.S. population. Such respected scientists as Michael Faraday and Louis Agassiz, as well as prominent artists, legislators, and social activists, participated in public debates about its validity and significance. Spiritualists regularly consorted with some of the historical figures who turn up in channeling events in the 1990s. During worship services held in 1843, for instance, Shakers living near Watervliet, New York, welcomed to their community Oliver Cromwell, Robespierre, Julius Caesar, Saint Patrick, George Washington, Catherine of Aragon, and even an Egyptian mummy. By the turn of the century, however, such lively manifestations of spiritualism were in decline. Most Americans interested in reincarnation and communication with the dead shifted their allegiance to the emerging field of parapsychology or to occult groups such as the Theosophical Society, which presented itself as the principal source of hidden wisdom emanating from a group of exalted beings—prophets, Bodhisattvas, and priests—who direct the future of humankind. Despite spiritualism's precipitous decline in popularity, small congregations carrying on the democratic tradition of mid-nineteenth-century spiritualism survive to the present, some operating under the aegis of organizations such as the National Spiritualist Association of Churches.[13]

American spiritualists believed strongly in the inherent divinity of the human race, which they saw moving steadily toward oneness with God. In 1854 the prominent spiritualist William Henry Channing argued that spiritualism represented the zenith of man's religious evolution. For Channing, spiritualism "asserts that love, reason, and creative power are really the Divine Life within us, which, by direct inspirations, is forming every spirit into an immortal image of the Infinite One." Just as today's channels certify that our world consists of far more than can be experienced on the material plane, so nineteenth-century spiritualists believed that the messages coming through them would banish all doubts about the reality of eternal life.[14]

A major goal of spiritualists was to bring science and religion into fruitful union. In part this reflected despair over the sectarianism of mainstream religions, which offered little hope of a unified vision of human destiny. Spiritualists were optimistic that science might succeed where religion had failed. Ultimately, however, most scientists proved unwilling to accept the holistic thinking advocated by spiritualists. This attempt to unify science and religion—or to push science in the direction of metaphysical questions—continues to be a hallmark of New Age thought. But while nineteenth-century spiritualism saw science as the potential savior of spirituality, the New Age now sees spirituality as the savior of science.

Historians have linked spiritualism to progressive political causes, including the struggle for women's rights, land reform, the abolition of slavery, and elimination of the death penalty. Having lost faith in the integrity of existing churches, spiritualists vested their hope in the intellectual and spiritual growth of individuals. "Every individual of sane mind ought to be left free to form his own opinions," wrote a spiritualist in 1854. This was the best alternative to established religion, which only served to "dwarf or deform their normal growth by the authority of creeds [and] the insemination of prejudices." An anonymous contributor to a spiritualist magazine argued that beneficial growth could take place if groups of people "would gather together in little circles, at stated intervals, with the bare idea of the possibility of their receiving communications from the world above."[15] The democratic sensibility of spiritualism was eroded after 1875 by the growth of the Theosophical movement, which emphasized secrecy, hierarchy, and the training of a spiritual elite. Today, channels are more likely to speak of self-actualization than of democracy, but they rarely miss an opportunity to assert the spiritual bankruptcy of all institutions predicated on hierarchy.

Similarities between spiritualism and channeling are tempered by important differences. Although spiritualists sometimes contacted Native American wise men and famous historical figures, most focused on communication with members of their clients' families who were recently deceased. Today, when so many Americans think of the nuclear family as a hothouse for pathology, few seem interested in contacting their dead relatives. If anything, they would rather deal with beings who were never human in the first place. Spiritualists hoped to reform Christianity, which they felt was corrupted by money and dogmatism. Channels, in contrast, express little interest in Christianity as such, although most see themselves as returning to the real values of Christianity—and, for that matter, to the underlying truth of all world religions. In a simpler age, spiritualism was a public spectacle as well as a philosophical movement. The shabby tricks of stage spiritualists—rapping noises, shaking furniture, and spurious ectoplasms—ultimately led to revelations of fraud that undermined the movement's credibility. As Kevin Ryerson noted during his workshop at the Omega Institute, channeling offers some degree of spiritual entertainment, but it can hardly compete with the megawatt amusements available to most Americans today.

The Christian concerns of the spiritualist movement live on in the practices of some contemporary channels. The Reverend Anna Swenson, a middle-aged woman from upstate New York, communicates regularly with the "Wise Ones," whom she describes as a group of souls joined like "strands of light intertwined in perfect harmony." At a public channeling event that she organized in 1991, Swenson arrived wearing a conservative floral skirt, a pastel blouse, and some simple jewelry. After announcing several upcoming workshops, she explained to newcomers that the Wise Ones would speak in a loud voice and that they usually request a few minutes of group meditation at the end of their visit. She pronounced a brief invocation, closed her eyes, and began to move her head slowly from side to side. She then began to speak in a style quite different from her remarks of only a few moments before. The sentences that tumbled out were over-enunciated and mechanical. As she talked, her head continued to pivot back and forth as if tracking an invisible tennis game. Her eyes blinked and twitched and sometimes rolled, revealing the whites. Periodically the Wise Ones paused in midsentence to say, "Give us a moment," after which they would return to their monologue.

Their message stressed that the personal, bodily aspect of human life is motivated by fears and desires. This is a necessary quality for survival in the material world, the Wise Ones said, but it interferes with the unfolding of a more spiritual self. We must therefore move beyond physical being and its desires to something on a higher level, laying the foundation for a totally spiritual existence when bodily life reaches its inevitable completion. Bringing the event to a close, the Wise Ones invited all to meditate, sitting with palms up in order to receive celestial energies. After ten minutes of silence, Anna emerged from her trance and switched on a recording of confectionery New Age music. Obviously moved, several members of the audience dabbed at their eyes with tissues. The message would not have been out of place in many Christian churches on a Sunday morning.

Anna Swenson's life story is marked by a persistent quest for a sense of connection to God. Brought up in a conservative Lutheran family, she explored other churches in search of a more vital form of worship. For a time, she attended an evangelical church but eventually became disillusioned with what she labeled its hypocrisy. After graduating from college with a degree in art, Anna moved to Los Angeles and then to San Francisco. Her career as an artist failed to prosper, however, and she drifted into new forms of spirituality then surfacing in the Bay Area. She studied at a center for psychics, then affiliated herself with a Hindu ashram. Eventually she found the Church of Religious Science, a New Thought denomination distantly related to Christian Science. At a Religious Science center in San Francisco, she worked with two women ministers who became key role models. At about this time, she came across *The Seth Material,* the first of several books by Jane Roberts. In 1963, long before channeling was a term in common use, Jane Roberts, a writer from Elmira, New York, began using trance states to contact Seth, who identified himself as a "personality without a body." Until her death in 1984, Roberts shaped the transcripts of her encounters with Seth into a series of books that have together sold more than a million copies. "The Seth books talk about your own power to create reality," Anna explained. "At that point, my life was out of control. I didn't have a clue as to where I was in the midst of it. So those two things, Religious Science and the Seth material, were an important awakening."

For several years, Anna trained as a Religious Science practitioner while taking classes in Transcendental Meditation on the side. Her interests gradually shifted from Religious Science to the Unity Church, another New Thought denomination. "Unity is more Jesus Christ-based than Religious Science," she explained. Anna was drawn to the emotional tone of Unity because she felt that she had exhausted the possibilities of Religious Science, which for her reached only the intellect. She enrolled at Unity's theological college in Missouri, but the death of her father and her own health problems interrupted her studies. Allergic to almost everything, she nearly died of anaphylactic shock on one occasion. Doctors pronounced her condition incurable. "They said that I should move to the desert and live in a stainless steel trailer," she explained. The diagnosis plunged her into a profound emotional and physical crisis. "I was just at my wit's end. Up to that point my conversations with God, or the God-Head as the Wise Ones call it, were 'Either heal me or take me, because I can't stand living like this.' And that night I totally surrendered. When I awoke, I knew that there was eternal life." Anna is convinced that the Wise Ones came to her at that moment, though she doesn't remember hearing them speak in words. In 1987 she was ordained a Unity minister and hired by a medium-sized congregation in an upstate New York city.

Anna's involvement with an established church should have been the happy conclusion to her search for stable employment and spiritual fulfillment. Yet it seems that her desire for deeper understanding led to restlessness and malaise. To revitalize her ministry, Anna began daily meditation. It was during these meditations that she began to feel the presence of the Wise Ones: "The energy would come over me and the muscles of my face would be moved. It was like a pulling in my throat and a pushing on my solar plexus. The energy was always beautiful and peaceful, though." When the Wise Ones haltingly came forth with their first word, it was "home." To Anna, this meant that she had reestablished a spiritual link initiated in her previous lifetimes. The Wise Ones identified themselves as spiritual teachers who were at the "next level of evolvement" from humanity. Their plan was to use Anna as their "generating station" through whom they could communicate to human beings.

Although Anna continued to serve as a minister, her channeling practice was too controversial for some members of the congregation. Eventually she resigned her position. Anna emphasized how she had agonized over the decision to forfeit the hard-won security of a regular job. Once free of the burdens of writing sermons and dealing with the church, however, she began to hold public channeling sessions and private consultations for which she received some compensation, although she appeared to be living in modest economic circumstances at the time of our meeting.

Anna saw her work as benefitting clients in two ways. The Wise Ones, she said, had emphasized that when she channels them, those present are bathed in spiritual energy. "The energy is the most important thing," she emphasized. "The Wise Ones have said that if someone's in their presence or in the presence of another true teacher, that person's essence or God-seed is awakened or accelerated." Yet the message is nearly as important as the energies that come with it. The Wise Ones themselves explained their message this way: "Our purpose is to bring the peace of God. The peace of God is God-experience. The peace of God is the experience of total acceptance, the experience of total oneness, the experience of no conflict within the consciousness of the individual."

Anna Swenson's approach to channeling preserves Christian idioms originally articulated by American spiritualists—notably, the spark of divinity within each of us, the necessary progression from body to spirit, and the inner peace that comes from the recognition of eternal life. Her autobiography, with its emphasis on the connection between crippling allergies and the emergence of the Wise Ones, also offers interesting parallels to the life of Mary Baker Eddy, who founded Christian Science in 1879. An invalid for many years, Eddy came under the influence of a prominent advocate of "mind cure" named Phineas Parkhurst Quimby. Quimby, who claimed to have healed himself of a vaguely defined neurasthenia through self-hypnosis, successfully cured Eddy of her ailments, thereby creating an eager disciple. Along with other proponents of what came to be called the New Thought movement, Eddy succeeded in making the transition from "therapy to theology" and thereby laying the foundation for a new church.[16] This pattern, referred to as the "power of the wounded healer" by people involved in alternative spirituality, is central to many channeling life stories today.

Conventional theologies typically offer a comprehensive view of good and evil that translates into a framework of moral guidelines. Yet discussions of morality are remarkably rare at channeling events, and it takes considerable probing to discover what channels and their clients think about such matters. When pushed, most channels reject formal systems of morality, arguing that they are inevitably supported by fear, which spawns violence and insensitivity. When people conquer fear and the sense of inadequacy that it produces, they begin to operate at a higher level of consciousness, one that transcends morality and ideas of divine punishment. Fixed notions of right and wrong are thought to stunt our spiritual growth by fostering a sense of separation. Among channels, separation carries the emotional resonance that sin holds for evangelical Christians. Separation causes us to lose sight of our oneness with the divine, thus furthering a destructive internal alienation. In the words of Deborah O'Neill, a channel from Santa Fe, inflexible notions of good and evil create "absolute separation, leaving you with little room to create, or move, or empower yourself—to become unconditional."

The origins of channeling's view of morality and the problem of evil can be traced, at least in part, to nineteenth-century spiritualists. In the spiritualist tract *Whatever Is, Is Right,* published in 1861, A. B. Child argues that because everything that happens is the will of a benevolent God, by definition humans cannot commit acts of evil. The channeled best-seller *A Course in Miracles,* today read in study groups across the nation, makes an identical case when it contends that cruelty and pain are nothing but figments of humanity's wounded imagination.

The absolute denial of evil was an extreme position, even for spiritualists. Most seem to have taken positions closer to that of

Andrew Jackson Davis, the most influential spiritualist thinker of his time. Davis accepted the reality of evil but argued that it represented only a transitory stage in the evolution of human-kind. Writing in 1873, he declared that war and other forms of human cruelty were steps in a "majestic march from the deep-est recesses of grossness and materiality to the highest eminences of refinement and spirituality." When today's channels talk about the process of spiritual "ascension," they speak of the same passage to divinity.

Spiritualists distrusted rigid moral rules. W. S. Courtney, fre-quent contributor to a journal called the *Spiritual Telegraph,* held that "man's inner nature, instead of being vicious and depraved, is plenary with every human excellence, beauty, and use." Courtney argued that the negativity of conventional Christian-ity, with its emphasis on sin and damnation, perverts the human soul, thus promoting acts of brutality. Moral rules, in other words, are the cause of human strife, not its cure.[17]

A channeling event that took place in 1993 in Santa Fe dem-onstrates the persistence of this hostile attitude toward morality. The event's hosts, both of whom appeared to be in their thir-ties, were a couple identified as Oberon and Lyra Alpha, repre-sentatives of the Church of Universal Spirit, an organization based in Colorado. Oberon wore loose-fitting trousers and a sweatshirt crossed by colored rays that were flecked with glit-ter. His wife Lyra was dressed more conservatively in black skirt, leggings, and blouse. A crucifix dangled from her neck. Two other members of their group helped out as the workshop un-folded. Oberon, Lyra, and their companions claimed to be ex-traterrestrials, walk-ins, who have taken on earthly bodies to as-sist the planet's awakening. In Oberon's words, their physical, emotional, and intellectual roots are in a "home outside this galaxy in nonlinear time/space." Seemingly at ease with their un-usual identity, they moved in a casual, loose-limbed way and chatted genially with members of the small audience.

In their opening remarks, Oberon and Lyra explained that Lyra channels several beings from distant galaxies, including a fifth-dimensional entity of indeterminate gender named Altair. Lyra relaxed her body and settled into trance. Altair emerged from her diminutive frame as an energetic, puckish voice with an accent reminiscent of British South Africa. "Ha! Good eve-ning," Altair greeted us. Turning to a gray-haired woman in the first circle of chairs, Altair said, "How be you, woman?" "Great," the woman responded. "Yes? You're having fun, huh?" Altair asked. Pointing to a man who prior to Lyra's trance had confessed that he was there only to accompany his wife, Al-tair said, "Even *he's* having fun, eh!" The man chuckled, then began an exchange with Altair that soon had Oberon and oth-ers laughing giddily. Lyra's animated face was creased by a warm smile as Altair clowned with the group.

Altair explained that our selves are more vast than we ever imagined. "You are a multidimensional being living simultane-ously on all dimensions back to God-All-That-Is," it said. "Oneness, that is who be you." Because we are multidimen-sional, the life that we think we are living right now is in fact an "illusionary holographic model," a game that we play to ac-quire truth needed for our journey. As divine beings, we can-not do wrong; we cannot go to hell because there is no hell: "You were made in the likeness and image of God. God-All-That-Is cannot make a mistake." In saying this, Altair articulated a position identical to that laid down by the spiritualist A. B. Child more than a century before.

As the small audience wrestled with the idea that everyday

life was only a mirage, Oberon interrupted Altair. He explained that these concepts are confusing because of the limitations of the English language. "English is a language of comparison and hierarchy," he said. "It was developed for commerce. But in the paradoxical universe in which we live, there is All-That-Is, and we are all of that. At the same time, we're a unique expression of that divinity, unlike anything else in the universe."

One participant, obviously perplexed, asked where ideas of personal responsibility fit into this model. Altair observed that the question was predicated on an assumption that humans are by nature evil. But since God made us, and God is love, there is no such thing as sin, no such thing as violence. "From the one-ness," Altair insisted, "everything was created. There is no death. There is no killing. It does not really exist." "So it doesn't mat-ter if you kill twenty people?" the skeptic persisted. Altair paused for a moment, then asked the questioner to repeat the following statement: "I formally rescind any and all vows, in this lifetime or in any other lifetime or embodiment, about needing to control myself and needing to protect others from myself. I rescind any vows that I am anything other than a loving being, and that I am not safe in the world, and that others are not safe in the world." Oberon gently intervened to explain that this process of rescind-ing vows was a new "technology" that freed important energies locked up in commitments to others. By letting go of them, he said, we're freeing up our energetic field. Oberon recommended that when seeking moral guidance, one should "access your inner knowing" rather than making decisions based on fear and doubt. It is pointless to follow the absolute rules typical of most belief systems, he said, because they create internal conflicts that lead to a "downward spiral of energy."[18]

Oberon shifted the evening's program toward his own channeling gift, the production of interdimensional tones. These sounds would produce "code adjustments" in our bodies, he explained, but the group had nothing to fear. After inviting everyone to stand, Oberon and Lyra positioned themselves around the first person in the small semicircle of participants. They were joined by the other members of their group, a stocky Asian-American man with long hair and a graying Anglo woman dressed in loose space-clothing similar to Oberon's. Oberon produced a wordless vocal tone that was soon echoed by the others. Their voices rose from a low rumble to a high wail, then dropped back into a lower register. There were occasional pops, chirps, hisses, and rhythmic pulses like soft bird calls, then moments of near silence punctuated only by faint grunts. The singers went from person to person, directing their sounds at each and stirring the air with vigorous arm movements. Sometimes the tones converged into a powerful wave of dissonance, producing an uncanny sense of physical vibration and heat, as if one's internal organs were being microwaved.

Inviting participants to sit again, Oberon led a brief exercise in guided imagery and then invited everyone to open their eyes to a new fifth-dimensional reality. Before bidding the group farewell, the channeled being named Altair explained that the participants were now ready to experience life in a new way, based on oneness rather than on limitation. "The karmic model has been shelved," Altair insisted. "Looking for what's wrong with you and trying to correct it is on the way out. So it is all good news."

Oberon and Lyra's channeling performance and the theological framework that it articulated were extreme even by the liberal standards of contemporary channeling. Relatively few channels concur with Oberon and Lyra's absolute denial of evil.

Instead, most acknowledge the human capacity to do harm and assert that such wrongdoing produces negative karma, which is repaid through painful experiences in subsequent lifetimes. One channel explained, for instance, that men who oppress women in one incarnation must work off their karma by being born as women in another. In fact, he asserted, some of today's most outspoken feminists were in their past lives men who oppressed women. Nevertheless, even believers in karmic justice prefer to focus on the coming age of spiritual union rather than speculate on the fate of the wicked.

Whatever their feelings about the nature of evil, most channels subscribe to an epistemological and moral relativism that leaves little room for prescriptive rules of conduct. Instead, they accept the more general precepts of the Golden Rule. They also embrace a diffuse but deeply felt commitment to protect the environment from further harm. More specific moral codes, however, are dismissed as inherently divisive. Deborah O'Neill, an unusually thoughtful channel, insisted on making a distinction between personal views of right and wrong and more encompassing systems of moral rules: "I'm willing to be responsible for labeling this as evil and labeling that as good. But I'm not willing to assume that there's a totally objective evil. It makes whole categories of people wrong, no matter what. You don't have room to create, or move, or empower yourself—to become unconditional." Her point was that morality encourages people to judge themselves and others too harshly, a tendency that conflicts with the self-affirming messages provided by contemporary channeling. At a deeper level, moral systems force us to live in a world of negativity—of can'ts and shouldn'ts, of fear and separation—that prevents the spread of a worldview based on unconditional love.[19]

A channeled lecture by David and Sasha Johnson made this point with special wit. The subject of their talk was sexuality, and David, drawing on the wisdom of Michael, the composite entity whom David and Sasha regularly channel, emphasized that judgment about sexual expression is misplaced. "Sex is an energy. From this point of view there are no value judgments and there are no morals and no ethics about sex. What we're working toward here is unconditional acceptance of your own sexuality and, of course, unconditional acceptance of everybody else's sexuality." When people in the audience asked about child abuse and rape, David admitted that they were undesirable—in his words, "very karmic"—because they lacked the element of consent. But he cautioned those present to beware of sexual morality, which is imposed by religions as a means of control. All forms of sexuality, he said, provide a soul with useful lessons. "If you choose to be somebody who likes to have sex with electric trains," David explained, "you're definitely going to feel out of place." Pausing until audience laughter had subsided, he concluded: "You'll go through all kinds of stuff about your self-esteem, and eventually you'll learn to accept that about yourself—that it's OK and that it's just a different way. It's not something to judge."

Although formal rules have no place in channeling, channels subscribe to an informal set of professional ethics. They must respect their clients' privacy, and they have an obligation to prevent clients from becoming overly dependent. The latter may be hard to resist, especially if emotionally fragile people are willing to pay for frequent counseling sessions. Yet professional channels insist that the creation of excessive dependence contradicts their principal aim, which is to lead clients to inner knowing. Another ethical responsibility is to "get in touch with the highest sources they possibly can," meaning that channels should distinguish personal opinions from information provided by spirits. Failure to do so may prompt the biting accusation that a channel is simply "channeling his ego."

A moral framework in which people are thought capable of creating their own reality and the existence of evil is routinely called into question provides two logical avenues for the interpretation of illness, poverty, and other forms of suffering. The first is that they occur because the victims cannot or will not envision the world in ways that protect them from misfortune. Calamity originates in a failure of individual attitude or thought. A newsletter distributed by a channel in upstate New York, for example, asserted that the national problem of homelessness is nothing but an illusion, "the last out-picturing of a form of mental and emotional poverty." Poverty exists, in other words, because poor people think impoverished thoughts. Belief in the ability of the mind to pluck hardship from a loving universe can be traced to the New Thought movement of the nineteenth century. Mary Baker Eddy, the founder of Christian Science, saw illness in these terms, and some of her contemporaries extended this line of thinking to account for poverty and its opposite.

The alternative is that victims of illness or misadventure have chosen their own fate, usually at a "deep soul level" beneath everyday awareness. The logic here is that reincarnating selves need a range of learning experiences in order to achieve spiritual maturity. The underlying eternal core of the self thus chooses certain challenges as part of its growth process.

In interviews, channels and their clients generally claimed to be reassured to learn that major life crises—financial insolvency, divorce, accident, serious illness—were really part of a larger plan subject to their personal control. A few, however, seemed uneasy with this way of looking at misfortune. Nancy Cohen, a Massachusetts channel committed to progressive politics, confided that this expression of New Age thought, which she labeled "spiritual Republicanism," sometimes troubled her. Nancy insisted that if she is present when human suffering takes place, then she, too, is there for a purpose. "It's my duty to help," she said. Yet even Nancy accepted that when, say, a woman is raped, she plays a part in the experience. "People are wronged. But one can ask, 'What will this woman who's been raped learn from this? Why was she put in this position?' She didn't choose it, but she *allowed* it at some level. Since it has happened, what's the reason for it?"

Handled clumsily, this perspective can produce statements of a moral relativism so profound that victims and perpetrators of crime become nothing more than "people working through their personal issues." Occasionally I heard stories about channels who used such logic in the guidance they delivered to clients. One woman, for instance, reported that a female relative trapped in a physically abusive marriage was told by a channel that she should endure her current suffering because it would restore karmic balance lost in a previous lifetime, during which she herself had been an abusive male. More common is the assertion that people are responsible for their own life-threatening disease. Speaking before a small group in Santa Fe, a channel struggled to explain the connection between illness and personal volition. "When a person has cancer," he said, "he is not *consciously* choosing the cancer. To tell the cancer-person that he has chosen the disease is New Age fascism. But on the *nonphysical level,* the individual God-force who has chosen the cancer-life has indeed chosen it deliberately for an experience." It is precisely this kind of victim-blaming, and the paralysis which it can induce, that is disparaged by critics of channeling.[20]

For channels, however, the point of saying that misfortune originates in the self is not to assign blame but to assert control. In this, they are explicitly reacting against the contemporary American cult of victimhood, which sanctifies persons or groups who can plausibly claim to have been wronged. Channeling's theological framework rejects victimhood because of its connotation of powerlessness, arguing instead that everyone suffers indignities on their way to higher consciousness. These painful episodes are important learning experiences, but nothing is gained by dwelling on them. We should simply acknowledge the pain and move on.[21]

Theodicy, the explanation of evil and misfortune, poses a challenge to any theological system. The Azande people of central Africa, whose attitude toward misfortune was famously described by the British anthropologist E. E. Evans-Pritchard, are practical in outlook, yet they are likely to account for illness or mishaps by attributing them to witchcraft. They understand, for example, that injury sometimes occurs while walking barefoot on the trails of their homeland. Nevertheless, one of Evans-Pritchard's Azande informants quickly concluded that witchcraft was the underlying cause of his own cut and infected foot. "What he attributed to witchcraft," Evans-Pritchard explains, "was that on this particular occasion, when exercising his usual care, he struck his foot against a stump of wood, whereas on a hundred other occasions he did not do so, and that on this particular occasion the cut, which he expected to result from the knock, festered whereas he had had dozens of cuts which had not festered."[22] Similarly, Americans understand that a disease such as cancer afflicts millions annually. But when faced with a diagnosis of cancer, they must answer the question, "Why do *I* have cancer and why *now?*" The merely statistical has become the urgently personal, thus demanding adequate explanation.

Some Americans find comfort in the belief that their illness, and the personal suffering that it causes, are all part of God's plan. Others make sense of their condition by laying blame on the corporations whose factories leak toxic wastes into the local drinking water. People drawn to channeling, however, believe that they author their own fate, that as divine actors their temporary setbacks and troubles must be part of a master plan ultimately of their own devising. Given these presuppositions, the conclusion that they are to some degree responsible for their own tribulations is inevitable. What is notable about this explanatory logic is its absolute denial of the social nature of human experience. The human actor faces the world alone and must assert control over his or her life as a solitary agent. The possibility that social forces affect one's health, safety, or economic well-being never enters into the picture, a fact that has profound implications for the attitudes toward community expressed by channels and their clients.

At first glance, the rejection of fixed moral rules by channels and others involved in alternative spirituality would seem to put them badly out of step with the rest of America. In a recent survey, seventy percent of a sample of middle-aged respondents declared themselves in favor of a "return to stricter moral standards." But underneath this statistic is a more ambiguous message. Almost half the conservative Protestants interviewed for the survey declared themselves uncomfortable with rigid moral codes, preferring instead to follow the dictates of their conscience.[23] This apparent contradiction signals a hope that relig-

ion will somehow foster a sense of personal ethics without re-
stricting individual freedoms.

The theology of channeling, then, brings together disparate
influences—among them, spiritualism's emphasis on the inherent divinity of humankind, the epistemological relativism of
contemporary academic and commercial discourse, collective
uneasiness about rigid morality, and a longstanding American
faith in the power of positive thinking to define our fate—to
produce a synthesis in which the self's sacred destiny prevails
over the arbitrary rules of society. Yet even as it claims to offer
a corrective to the sense of separation that afflicts so many people today, channeling's portrait of humans as autonomous and
god-like agents throws up a subtle barrier between self and
other. "We must each take full responsibility for our own happiness," channels say, a view that despite its apparent optimism
reduces the passions and predicaments of social life to a vast
game, or, as the entity Altair would have it, to "an illusionary
holographic model." From this cosmic hallucination the self
emerges triumphant. Ultimately, however, it emerges alone.

4

MASTERING SELF-EXPANSION

People drawn to channeling, either as producers or consumers of channeled information, pride themselves on independence of mind. Most reject attempts to codify their beliefs or to formalize techniques for acquiring spiritual knowledge, preferring instead to pick and choose from among the ideas that circulate in the workshops and individual counseling sessions in which they participate, thus crafting a distinctive, personal idea of channeling practice. Yet there must be a counterweight to these centrifugal tendencies, some shared experiential core, that prevents channeling from spinning off into a thousand fragments. How are channeling's theological axioms and experiential landmarks communicated, learned, and mapped onto individual lives? If, as the English critic John Ruskin asserted, education is not "teaching people to know what they do not know" but instead "teaching them to behave as they do not behave," by what means do channels learn to behave as channels?

An opportunity to gain some purchase on these questions arose in 1993 in the form of a workshop designed to teach basic techniques for contacting spirit guides. The organizer of the two-day class was Deborah O'Neill, a Santa Fe channel whom I had interviewed two years before. Bright and articulate, Deborah had a down-to-earth manner that inspired confidence. When I called her to inquire about the workshop, she proved open to the idea of an anthropologist participating in the two-day class.

On a luminous Saturday morning in September, Deborah welcomed a dozen pupils to the suburban-style ranch house that she shared with her husband and young daughter. The house was decorated with pieces of her sculpture and glasswork, some exploring shamanic themes in an expressionist style. Beyond the living room was a bright kitchen, where her daughter's school drawings hung from a refrigerator door. Contemplative music, hinting of Tibetan monasteries or desert vision quests, played softly in the background. As participants in the workshop bivouacked around the room on pillows and a sofa, several placed crystals on the floor directly in front of themselves.

The eleven seekers whom I joined for Deborah's class were representative of channeling audiences in northern New Mexico: predominantly middle-aged, white, and female (eight women versus three men), although the group also included an Asian-American man and an African-American woman. There was an expedition outfitter who had spent years in the Yukon, a computer technician who worked at Los Alamos National Laboratory, a housewife, and a professional counselor who used psychic information to enhance her practice. Some regularly sought Deborah's spiritual guidance in private sessions, whereas others scarcely knew her. The common denominator was a desire to "open to the inner voice," as one woman put it.

Deborah picked up this theme as she oriented the group to

what was to happen during the two-day class. An advocate of conscious channeling, Deborah said that her plan was to help the group "bring normal reality and paranormal reality into a place where they're one, where it feels like miracles are how we live our life." Most people are afraid to let those two great rivers—thought and intuition—flow together, she emphasized. They edit themselves, suffer from performance anxiety, and invent a hundred reasons not to heed their inner knowing. The goal for the weekend was to allow all present to feel the inner magnificence that they so frequently deny. Those seeking to lose themselves in submission to some higher being had best find another guide into the world of channeling, she warned. "We're here to honor ourselves, to understand ourselves as God-present beings, absolutely open to the totality of the light," Deborah insisted. "My personal goal is to make the shift to channeling less dramatic rather than more." With these remarks, she made it clear that her aim was to introduce the group to the powerful beings inside themselves, not somewhere else. "Think of it this way. You open up, and you get a bigger picture. Well, what's going to be the most important thing in your bigger picture? It's probably going to be you."

Her personal ally for the duration of the workshop was a spirit—or, as Deborah put it, an "energy format"—named Dwahl Khul or, more informally, DK, whom she has channeled for many years. (The name Dwahl Khul is a slight alteration of Djwhal Khul, The Tibetan, a source channeled by Alice Bailey and other Theosophists beginning in the 1920s.) Although DK's energy has a distinctive quality, Deborah said, she does not think of it as a force beyond herself. Rather, it is something thoroughly integrated into her being. DK had helped her move beyond the sense of personal limitations that had once plagued her.

She fielded questions from the group. In response to a query about whether one should channel with eyes open or closed, Deborah said that it varied according to each person's needs. She found that closed eyes produced deeper meditation, which enhanced her channeling response, but for others this wasn't necessary. When giving private readings for clients, she had discovered that some like eye contact. Others prefer that she keep her eyes closed "so that they could go into their deep private space with the channeled information." She emphasized that it was ultimately up to each participant to decide what worked. "Anything that you come up with for *you* is important to maintain, even if it's different from what I would do," she stressed.

Deborah announced that it was time to move into a deeper place, "a place where we know that our greater selves are guiding us and helping us move into the state of consciousness that we call channeling." She sat quietly for a moment, then began to talk in the channeled voice of DK, louder and with more careful diction than her everyday speech. "Channeling is an opening of the heart," DK said to the group. "Allow yourself to use your gifts. Each one of you chooses a particular pathway. You are totality. You are God, operating on a particular resonance." DK assured everyone that there was no need to fear dark forces because channeling brings one to "a more glorified, amplified, God-present state," a place of perfect safety.

Deborah and DK led the group on a guided meditation to the inner self. We were told to envision a beautiful place in nature and open the senses to all of its qualities—smells, sounds, colors, textures. We were then to collect the energy that emerged from the door of our heart, energy that DK said was "personally symbolic of your open, clear channel." Deborah's steady voice brought the group out of its meditation and back into the room.

She asked members of the class to share their experiences, especially any symbolic images that might have presented themselves.
Mark, a visitor from Massachusetts, described his image as a heart
with wings. "Then I sort of breathed life into it and it began to
pulsate with heart energy." He reported that this led him to images of the Ascended Masters. Compared to the elaborate, kaleidoscopic images reported by Mark and other participants, the luminous inverted triangle that I had discovered seemed ordinary,
but Deborah assured me that it was an alchemical symbol of God
coming to earth.

To move the class into a deeper meditative state for the next
exercise, Deborah rubbed a soft mallet around the rim of a glass
bowl, producing a powerful tone. She moved us through a se-
quence of imaginary lakes: the Pool of Power, the Pool of Clarity, the Pool of Love, the Pool of Trust. After the meditation,
Deborah debriefed the class. Participants reported strong feelings of well-being, visions of colored energies pouring into their
bodies, and even encounters with mysterious human or animal
figures. Still, many seemed uncertain about how to interpret the
imagery or even whether they should invest much significance
in it. Deborah insisted that their intuitive gifts were stronger
than they realized and that visions such as these could help them
access potent forms of inner knowing.

During a lunch break members of the class sat in the brilliant
sunlight of Deborah's backyard. They were a friendly, animated
group, and as they talked about their lives it was evident that
most had families, conventional jobs, and varied life experiences. Their casual discussion about the workshop suggested
that they saw channeling as a way to broaden themselves by
pushing into uncharted personal terrain.

In the afternoon, Deborah set the group to work writing personal invocations that would establish the proper mind-set for channeling. It was important, she said, to state one's goals. Some people want to use channeling to encourage physical healing; others want to contact *devas* or earth spirits. She noted that her own invocation has gradually shifted from a focus on contacting a specific spirit guide toward a more expanded approach, forging a link to "the super-essential light field or the greater self of all greater selves." Here she referred to her conviction that the self is an infinitely expansive force that when stripped of the baggage of daily life is really a field of light.

The group shared its invocations, most of which expressed a desire to connect to the vast store of knowledge available in the higher self. The invocation of one woman went as follows: "In a state of knowingness of my profound power, I ask to communicate with visual and symbolic information available to me in a form healing to the body, soul, and spirit, through my being-ness and through my energy patterns transferred by these hands to awaken, love, and serve." Another asked for "the most profound awareness of my greater self to guide me to and through self-trust and worthiness, in unconditional love." The invocations showed the influence of Deborah's gentle pressure, which pushed the group away from a search for grandiose spirits similar to J. Z. Knight's channeled entity, Ramtha, and toward a more humanistic form of spiritual connection that stressed the channel's own inherent divinity.

Deborah recontacted DK, who offered pointers on learning to channel. He encouraged people to trust the feelings that came when they opened up to channeling and not to worry about whether these impressions made sense on some everyday level. Our goal, he said, was to get the simple truth, however it manifested itself—as words, images, sounds, or movements. Information comes from the "realms of light" and, through the channeling process, is transformed in such a way that it "vibrates your emotional, mental, and physical vehicles." To get to this state of spiritual openness, Deborah had told us earlier, apprentice channels should develop their own ritual. After the recitation of an invocation, the ritual might include burning sage, ringing Tantric bells, or holding a powerful crystal. "Channeling," she said, "is really a shamanic rite. A shaman is someone who goes into other worlds to help and assist, to retrieve information or healing for someone else. For me, that's exactly what channeling is all about."[1]

Fifteen years earlier, I had witnessed a half-dozen shamanic rituals while living among the Aguaruna Indians of the Peruvian Amazon. The shaman, or *iwishín,* who presided over these rituals was a wiry man named Yankush, my neighbor for more than a year. Because Aguaruna shamans control powerful forces, they are major players in the intricate politics of a society disturbed by frequent threats of violence. The Aguaruna believe that shamans can kill as well as cure, so their behavior is scrutinized closely. The constantly shifting balance between their allies and enemies—they inevitably have both—determines whether they live to enjoy old age or die in a murderous ambush on some lonely trail.

It is hard to convey the intensity of the emotions evoked when Yankush treated patients, usually sick kinsmen from nearby villages. Like other Aguaruna shamans, Yankush achieved a trance state by drinking a concoction made from the *ayahuasca* vine, a powerful hallucinogen, that was mixed with several other ingredients about which he was extremely secretive. In the visions summoned by the hallucinogenic mixture, he looked for evidence of the sorcery that had ravaged his patient's health. The nauseous brew would cause him to retch noisily and writhe in pain as his stomach twisted into knots. Often, the patient moaned and begged for relief. The patient's relatives shouted words of encouragement, as well as demands that Yankush name the sorcerer who had harmed their loved one. "Tell us who he is so that we can kill him," they often insisted. Gathering his energies, Yankush would perform healing songs whose words moved deftly between concrete observations about the illness in front of him and poetic descriptions of his struggle against sorcerers. The songs were so dense with metaphors that they nearly defied translation. Shared symbols based on Aguaruna mythology and rainforest flora and fauna were soft clay in the capable hands of Yankush, who manipulated them to transform his patient's sense of reality and thereby to achieve a form of healing. This sophisticated control of symbols did not come easily, for shamans such as Yankush endure years of personal sacrifice to master their art. Among the Aguaruna, and elsewhere in the world, shamans need decades to learn complicated healing songs—in some societies, a feat of memory equivalent to memorizing the Old Testament.[2]

Deborah O'Neill was hardly alone in making an explicit comparison between channeling and the practices of shamans like Yankush. Identification with tribal shamanism holds immense appeal because it conjures up romantic images of sweat lodges, ancient tribal wisdom, and control of mystical powers. But do channeling and shamanism really have much in common?

The answer to this question is complicated by disagreement among experts about how shamanism itself should be defined. One widely accepted definition holds that shamans use trance to embark on what they perceive as a perilous soul-journey, usually with the goal of doing battle with sorcerers or leading a sick person's errant soul home to safety. Within this framework, the key diagnostic features of shamanism are trancing, soul-travel, and mastery of alien spirits. Channeling satisfies the first part of the definition but not the rest, for channels rarely claim to go on soul-journeys, at least while channeling, nor do they see themselves as controlling entities in a purposeful way. In strictly formal terms, channeling bears a stronger resemblance to spirit possession or mediumship, a practice in which people serve as passive vehicles for visiting spirits. In some societies, mediums control the spirits who possess them. In others, they are unwilling vessels, and their role as spirit-hosts is seen as an affliction. But in either case, spirits come to human mediums rather than vice versa.

Although the distinction between shamanism and spirit possession is plain in theory, practitioners show little concern for anthropologists' tidy classifications. Among the Tungus people of Siberia, whose language gave us the word "shaman," healers routinely experience magical soul-flights *and* possession. Shamanistic practices prove just as diverse in other societies. Confronted by the wide range of techniques used by shamans around the world, one expert has proposed that shamanism be defined as broadly as possible. "A shaman," he writes, "is an inspired prophet or healer, a charismatic religious figure, with the power to control the spirits, usually by incarnating them." Within the terms of this broadened definition, American channels seem to qualify as shamans.[3]

The trouble with formal definitions is that they say little about context. A botanist identifies thyme largely on the basis of its flower structure. A gardener, in contrast, will insist that thyme is a useful herb when it grows obediently in its proper place and a vicious weed when it threatens to strangle her favorite delphiniums. Context is no less important in social life. When we compare the social context of American channeling to that of shamanism, the similarities begin to fade. Among tribal and peasant peoples, shamanism takes place in a world of extraordinary social density. The players in communal religious dramas share a wealth of collective experience. They have been raised on the same myths, seen the same rituals, tilled identical fields, witnessed the same moral crises. Their world is crosshatched with common dreams and shared meanings, just as it is with smoldering resentments and petty jealousies. In this setting, the *feel* of shamanism could hardly be more different from that of channeling.

Shamans such as Yankush manipulate highly specific, shared symbols that shape the understanding of a tightly-knit group of kinsmen and allies. Much of the discussion that takes place in Aguaruna healing sessions is focused precisely on family disputes and other particulars of life in a face-to-face society that lacks centralized authority. The information that emerges in shamanic trances may ratify the local status quo or challenge it, but its impact is always political in the broadest sense of the word. In contrast, a typical American channeling session involves people who come together for a single event—a lecture, a weekend workshop, or perhaps a personal counseling session lasting for an hour. The members of a channeling audience are, of course, likely to hold vaguely similar ideas about personal growth and the nature of the spirit world. Nevertheless, the symbolic vocabulary of channels is dominated by abstract references into which clients can read whatever they like. Consider, for example, the language of a channeling session in Santa Fe. Speaking for a being named Andora, who hails from the Pleiades, the channel declared: "The accelerated frequencies we are now beaming in your direction are for the purpose of healing, of alignment and attunement of your hearts, the desires of the God within you. For you see, the physical body must also receive the frequencies of oneness which match your deepest heart's desires. Within the Pleiades, we are assisting the earth and humanity to integrate accelerated frequencies."

In comparison to the language of Yankush's healing songs, which are thick with specific references to local history, the natural world, and Aguaruna mythology, Andora's speech is nebulous, even bureaucratic. Phrases such as "frequencies of oneness," "alignment and attunement," and "the God within you" can be read many different ways. In fact, that is their goal, for more specific concepts would either be lost on the audience or rejected as an attempt to impose a particular belief system, which from a New Age perspective is entirely unacceptable. During his Omega Institute workshop, Kevin Ryerson was so anxious to avoid looking like someone who promoted specific beliefs that he invited potential skeptics to interpret channeling as a poetic phenomenon rather than as something real. Any Amazonian shaman who suggested that his clients were free to interpret the violent world of sorcery as mere poetry would be dismissed as a madman.

Although the similarities between American channeling and shamanism in intimate tribal settings wither under close scrutiny, they hold up slightly better when the comparison is to forms of spiritual healing that have emerged in the cities of the developing world. In urban Brazil, where African, Amerindian, and European cultures fertilize a lush garden of spiritualist practices, some mediums exhibit the vague language and business-like attitude of North American channels. Weekly events held by Chico Xavier, one of Brazil's best-known mediums, are regularly attended by hundreds. Xavier spends most of his sessions communing with spirits while sitting in a closet. He periodically hands out messages to an officious secretary, who then delivers them to anxiously waiting clients. Xavier never lays eyes on most of the people for whom he is channeling. He probably hasn't the time, because in addition to his active practice as a spiritual counselor he has also channeled a sixteen-volume series describing the inner workings of a celestial community that hovers over Rio de Janeiro. At healing sessions sponsored by practitioners of Umbanda, a spirit-possession cult blending African and European traditions, patients are sometimes given numbers and asked to wait their turn until a busy medium can get to their case. Elsewhere in Latin America, urban shamans and healers may treat scores of patients a day in a setting as impersonal as any doctor's office in the United States.[4]

Against this background, the claim of channels that they are modern-day shamans becomes slightly more convincing. Like their counterparts in urban areas of the Third World, American channels draw on the symbolic resources of tribal tradition, recycling them in a generic form suitable for a mass audience. Nevertheless, contemporary American channels are far more likely to identify with healers in remote rainforests or desert villages than with shamans and mediums working in the slums of Rio, Bogotá, or Manila. The tumult of urban life is simply too hard to reconcile with channeling's image of itself as a path to ancient wisdom and renewed intimacy with nature.

To help the group of apprentice channels overcome performance anxiety, Deborah and DK assigned an intuitive task. We had been instructed to bring to the workshop an object "invested with personal energy." The group heaped the items—an old blanket, jewelry, a half-dozen crystals, a set of car keys, and a Swiss Army knife—in the center of the room. Each then had to pick something at random and channel information about its owner, whose identity was not to be revealed until the task was completed.

DK explained that everyone experiences a channeling state of consciousness at some point in their lives, perhaps in a moment of creativity or insight. Essentially, he said, it consists of opening to another reality that lies beyond the conscious mind. "Channeling is a process of translating information and energy that is nonarticulate, that operates in the realm of light, and bringing those symbols into communicable formats," DK explained. To channel, one simply learns to recover those messages and then translate them faithfully into whatever form of expression seems most appropriate: words, music, or movements. "What you are here to do is to trust yourself," DK said.

Janet, one of the more confident participants, volunteered to go first. After performing her invocation, she slowly developed a story about the object that she picked from the pile, the tattered blanket. "This blanket has traveled on a long journey to come to you," Janet said. "It's related to a new life that's filled with joy and a movement away from an older sadness. And it seems that you might be questioning how all this will go. That question is a hindrance to your enjoyment of where you're going." As she spoke, tears welled up in the eyes of a woman named Cora, who proved to be the blanket's owner. Cora commented that Janet had captured her personal situation well, and she thanked her for the insight. And so it went for the entire group. Anne, who channeled the pocketknife that I had contributed to the pile of objects, felt in it a connection to "someone with strong heart-energy who likes to hide it with skepticism," a plausible description of a visiting social scientist.

When it was my turn, I chose one of the crystals and nervously turned it over in my hands. Closing my eyes, I tried to capture the diffuse energies that DK had told us to seek when channeling. To my surprise, I saw an incendiary landscape of southwestern mesas that evoked a sense of regret followed by a feeling of reconciliation. When I finished describing this sensation, Donna, an attractive black woman from the Albuquerque suburbs, identified herself as the crystal's owner. "You were right," she said. "I had a dream like that a few months ago, and there was a lot hanging on it. I had to reconcile myself with it." Deborah jumped in to explain that intuition was a muscle that only needed exercise. "Don't worry if it feels like you're making it all up, because you're not," she said reassuringly. Deborah's supportive comments fostered an atmosphere in which participants were free to explore their intuition without fear of failure or ridicule.

As the afternoon drew to a close, Deborah assigned homework. Everyone in the class was to write out his or her invocation and refine it if necessary. For the next day's class, participants were to bring a picture—a photograph, a magazine clipping, a postcard—that had some personal meaning. Then she channeled DK, who announced that this day had been an important opening for the entire group: "You're much, much greater than even your expanded self thinks that it is. You are loved by God-presence. You *are* God-presence." By that DK apparently meant that we had connected to the elemental forces of the universe in ways that would broaden our perspective and self-understanding. "Whenever an opening takes place, there is a consequential sense of becoming more than you thought you were. Sometimes that's hard to deal with. So be very gentle with yourself and trust the deeper truth that you're even more than you think." These comments skillfully weave together several threads of channeling's theology. In addition to emphasizing our divine nature, DK implies that we share a kaleidoscopic internal multiplicity. Each person's hidden inner selves—the source of the voices, sounds, emotions, or images accessed by channeling—are somehow more sacred, more connected to the forces that drive the universe, than is the everyday self. To bring these fragments of the inner self into focus is to infuse life with magic.

The group straggled into the living room late the next morning. Two members of the class had fallen by the wayside, but the rest seemed ready to press on. After some informal discussion about Deborah's relationship with her entity DK and other matters, she settled into the channeling state. Deborah and DK led the group through a meditative search for a personal sound or tone that would "bring our bodies of light to their highest vibratory frequency." Soon the room vibrated with low Tibetan growls, upward-spiralling glissandos, and weird yipping sounds. The point of this, according to DK, was to attune the inner self to any kind of information that might produce insight. "Let yourself relate to whatever occurs in your environment in channeling," DK said. "When channeling for someone else, let yourself ask questions if there is confusion. Let yourself respond to a feeling that you have of discomfort within them. Let yourself respond to your own discomfort, for in this state of consciousness you can be extremely sensitive. We are not presenting channeling as an experience that takes you wholly and completely out of a situation. We are suggesting that channeling and the state of consciousness can bring you more wholly and completely *into* the situation, the environment, the experience, the exchange."

When DK had finished speaking through Deborah, she paired off the participants in the first of a series of channeling exercises designed to put DK's suggestions into practice. I found myself facing Steven, an amiable San Franciscan who had traveled to New Mexico to take part in the workshop. The first assignment was to use a picture to develop a channeled story that shed light on our partner's personal circumstance. Steven had chosen a whimsical photograph, obviously cut from a magazine, of Santa Claus in an easy chair. After performing my invocation, I closed my eyes and waited for something to present itself. The sensations were indistinct, and all I could muster was a series of disjointed impressions. "I sense warmth and a sense of humor," I told Steven. "There's something about a family there too. I can't quite make it out. There's deep caring but perhaps separation as well." As I struggled with the translation of vague feelings and impressions into words, I wondered whether I was simply engaged in a deductive process of connecting the curious picture to what little I knew about Steven: that he was Asian-American and a recent widower, that he made his living by providing therapeutic massage and other forms of "bodywork," and so on. When I later mentioned this to Deborah, she laughed good-naturedly. "The doubts are starting, eh?" she asked. For Deborah it did not matter what the process was called—channeling, intuition, unconscious inference—as long as it led to insight. Suddenly growing serious, she emphasized that one should make no claims about the information unless it came as part of a true shift in consciousness. "If you're not in another state of consciousness, if you're not God-present, then you're fooling yourself by saying that it's channeling." The state of "God-presence" meant stepping past everyday concerns into a condition of openness to influences beyond those encompassed by linear thought processes. "I see channeling as good training for unconditionality," Deborah said, "because you have to let go completely. You have to let go of initial superficial judgments of who somebody is."

As the exercises continued, it became clear that stripped of rhetoric about Ascended Masters or vibrations from the Pleiades, channeling could be an effective transactional tool. The channel's words, however ordinary, strike a chord with others, who proceed to interpret them according to their own preoccupations, which may eventually nudge them toward a new understanding of their situation. "The person for whom you're channeling may hear your message in a completely different way," Deborah explained. "When that happens, you have to let go and allow the other person's interpretation." She referred to this chain of events as "trinitization": insight cycles from the channel's higher self to the channel, then to the client. This evokes new questions from the client, repeating the cycle until the reading is completed.

Such exchanges reveal striking parallels to the form of divination practiced by the Ndembu people of Zambia. Ndembu diviners shake a score of symbolic objects in a millet basket and then decipher patterns that form as the objects heap together. Ndembu diviners balance their intuition, which they understand as having a mystical origin, against a shrewd reading of the family conflicts that usually lie behind their clients' anxiety. Through this subtle, interactive process, skilled diviners succeed in "revealing the hidden," as the Ndembu put it. Although the idioms used by an American channel are different from those of a Ndembu diviner, both aim for transactional revelation. For that matter, so do most Western psychotherapists.[5]

In the final hours of the workshop, Deborah tried to move the group toward deeper understanding by opening herself to sources other than DK. She introduced us to an angel named Rafael and a squeaky-voiced fairy called Elicia. During a rest break, someone asked Deborah whether channeling should be considered a means of tapping into something beyond the self. Deborah giggled, referring to this idea as the "reception deception." "If you believe that you are receiving something from outside yourself," she said, "then you've denied and diminished yourself."

The final exercise called for each participant to channel a closing statement. A few people had already begun to contact spiritual sources with names and personalities. For instance, one woman channeled as if she were speaking in the voice of an un-named earth spirit. "I speak to you from the earth as a mother who sees you all as having the capability to help my children grow. And I encourage you to use this opening, this gift, to give other people a chance to see themselves as you see them." The rest of the class let the words rise up from the channeling zone, wherever it was. Most statements encouraged the group to carry on with channeling in the coming years. One man congratu-lated us for learning to expand our vision of the universe. "We are much bigger than our narrow perceptions allow us to be-lieve," he said. "So hold that expanded vision of this weekend's experiences as we move forward." In keeping with the atmos-phere of the past two days, Deborah and the others murmured words of support after each channeling performance, no matter how limited or halting.

When everyone had spoken, Deborah reconnected to DK, who offered personal comments for each participant and ratified the great strides made by everyone in the class. DK predicted that Steven, the man from San Francisco, would now be far more in touch with inner knowledge. "What you are going to find unfolding before you is a more significant sense of being whole, of being absolutely on target with your intuition and with your intuitive sensitivity. Trust what comes through you." DK insisted that a great change had taken place in everyone present. "What's happened this weekend is that you have begun to accept that there is a greater being present within you. This channel-opening will facilitate your every step." "For indeed," DK concluded, "you are a clear and open channel, or you would not have come here and experienced yourself." As Deborah brought the workshop to a close, she urged the participants to "experience the magnificence of being simply who you are, which is more than you ever imagined."

Eight weeks after the workshop, I contacted three of the participants to see whether DK's promises of lasting impact had proved accurate. All said that they were channeling easily and often, although still only for themselves or for close friends. Sandy, the computer technician, reported that she was in contact with a range of energies, mostly female, including an elderly Native American woman with healing powers. She and three other women from the workshop continued to meet weekly, helping one another to refine their channeling ability. Sandy now felt so confident that she planned to give channeled readings to several of her friends as a Christmas present.

Marilyn, a state employee, explained that she did not experience channeling as a connection to named beings but rather as an opening to "clear energies" that made her feel powerful. "I get really valuable information about myself," she said. The positive results of the workshop were a great relief after several years of involvement with a conservative religious group. Although Marilyn admired the group's teachings, she eventually became disillusioned with its insistence that only designated prophets could receive religious insight. "My perspective after channeling is that it's all there if you ask for it," she said. Deborah O'Neill's channeling class inspired her to move past her former congregation's narrow attitudes, which stood in the way of her personal development.

Jim, the expedition outfitter, reported that the class had opened him to a new awareness of the world's spiritual resources. He now regularly contacted an entity named Andrew, whom he identified as a "being of light," as well as other sources that were less clearly defined. Some of what he received appeared to come from outside of himself; the rest was clearly from a deeper part of his own understanding. All of it was, in Jim's words, "very wise," and he was hopeful that it would eventually become integrated into his everyday experience. "The part-of-me bit I want to bring more into myself," he explained. "As for the other stuff, I don't know quite what to think."

The accounts of these three participants imply that each had applied Deborah O'Neill's lessons in slightly different ways to suit diverse needs and temperaments. Sandy, for instance, experienced channeling as contact with identifiable spirits, Marilyn as a connection to more abstract forces. None seemed especially interested in developing elaborate histories for the powers they encountered in the channeling state. This probably reflected Deborah's influence. Her class defined channeling as a process of personal expansion rather than as a search for awesome spiritual beings living at a higher level than the self. A how-to class run by someone else might have pushed the group more vigorously in the direction of contacts with fully developed, named beings.

The common denominator in Deborah's workshop was a connection to "energies," a term used almost universally in channeling and related spiritual practices. Energy is a perfect organizing concept because it is both all-encompassing and ambiguous. Like the spirit world itself, energy is everywhere yet difficult to see. Its elusive, mysterious quality lends itself to metaphysical speculation. Each of us has experienced energy in palpably physical forms: sound, vibrations, light, heat, gravity. By bridging scientific and spiritual approaches to the world, energy offers a way to bring everything together in a grand synthesis. "Ultimately, everything is energy," channels often say. Because energy is everything, it is also nothing very specific, which makes it a perfect vehicle for creating shared meaning among spiritual individualists. The chief lesson of the channeling class was that these omnipresent energies are texts that we can learn to read, texts that ultimately offer clues to the self. By reading them, we assimilate new identities, becoming wiser and more powerful in the process. Jim, who as an expedition guide had struggled through some of the most hostile terrain on earth, felt that his new-found gift had greatly increased his ability to gather the messages dancing around him. "There's a lot more energy out there than we think, and it's all information," he said. "We can pick our way through it to find our own wisdom."

The comments of Jim and his classmates, who now contentedly create their own wisdom, exemplify channeling's precarious position in the borderland between religion and therapy. In comparison to the world's ancient religions, which routinely demand years of diligent work before practitioners can fully comprehend even the simplest of sacred truths, channeling offers an abstract and rather ambiguous language that can be mastered in a few days. The altered state associated with channeling is easily learned, although it presumably would take months or years to refine it to the level demonstrated by some accomplished channels. Once grasped, channeling's techniques and concepts can quickly be reshaped into a personal philosophy and immediately put to work decoding the mysteries of self. Channeling welcomes everyone because it demands and presupposes little. Its philosophical and theological thinness is, from this perspective, an asset rather than a liability.

Channeling's flexibility can be seen as the pinnacle of a mode of thought that the philosopher Charles Taylor has called "subjectivist expressionism," an outlook that values above all else "self-expression, self-realization, self-fulfillment, [and] discovering authenticity."[6] When taken to an extreme, Taylor observes, subjectivist expressionism hurtles toward the omega point of absolute emptiness. The uncharitable observer might conclude that the apprentice channels trained in Deborah O'Neill's workshop have already bought a one-way ticket to Taylor's subjectivist void. But we should keep their current passion for exploring inner space in perspective. The biographies of other Americans, especially members of the Baby Boom generation, reveal considerable restlessness with respect to religious loyalties. This emerging national pattern suggests that within a few years, Jim, Marilyn, and Sandy are likely to have moved on to other religious venues, quite possibly to groups where personal agendas are balanced by a sense of altruism and collective purpose.[7] Marilyn had been part of one such congregation before learning to channel, and her rejection of it reflected a need for independence and emotional self-sufficiency. It would not be surprising if in a few years she felt confident enough to return to a conventional church of some kind. For now, however, she needs to explore her own divinity. "In my sessions working with Deborah," Marilyn said, "DK told me that you can't go by somebody else's rules on sexuality or the types of food that you eat or how to live your life. You have to go by what works for you. My choice has been to step outside the organization frame of mind. As soon as I made that choice, I felt the expansion."

5

TOWARD SACRED ANDROGYNY

The self-expansion that Marilyn and others pursue through channeling routinely takes them into unusual gender territory. Although women were prominent in the rise of channeling in the 1970s and 80s, for instance, most of the entities they channeled were identified as male. In the 1990s, channels report more frequent contacts with feminine or sexually ambiguous beings, and they emphasize the important role that spiritual gender-crossing can play in broadening people's views of their own internal multiplicity. Their increasing self-consciousness about the connection between gender and spirituality parallels the rise of gender-focused religious movements elsewhere in America.

In mainstream Christian denominations, some women not only demand a larger role in day-to-day participation and decision-making but also seek representation in liturgy through the introduction of feminine symbols such as the biblical figure Sophia, a female personification of God.[1] Even among evangelical Christians who see men as the biblically ordained leaders of home and church, feminist ideals

have subtly influenced teachings about marriage and family. At
the same time, and partially in response to the emergence of
women-centered forms of spirituality, thousands of men now
flock to revivals organized by the Promise Keepers, an evangelical fellowship dedicated to helping men "reclaim their man-
hood" within a Christian moral framework. The most dramatic
expressions of gender-focused spirituality take place farther from
the mainstream, in ecofeminist workshops, neopagan covens,
Goddess seminars, men's drumming groups, and, in smaller
numbers, communities that experiment with nontraditional
family arrangements and sexual practices.[2]

This is hardly the first time that a preoccupation with gender
has arisen in American religion. In the nineteenth century,
groups such as the Shakers and the Oneida Community experimented with novel family structures and approaches to sexuality,
ranging from total celibacy to free love, in an attempt to offer a
level of personal freedom denied them by the wider society. Although nineteenth-century spiritualists were not prominent
among those advocating novel rearrangements of family structure, they were deeply committed to the emergence of women
from their subordinate status in Christian churches. At the very
least, spiritualism offered female mediums an escape from the
straitjacket of social convention. Between 1854 and 1861, for
example, a former invalid from Vermont named Achsa Sprague
held audiences spellbound with her inspirational lectures, presented while she was deep in trance. Her fame as a public speaker
opened to her a life unknown to most women of the time. She
traveled extensively, acquired independent means, and felt free
to decline offers of marriage from admirers. Other women found
that spiritualism allowed them even bolder forms of self-expression. The English medium Annie Fairlamb regularly produced a

spirit named Minnie, who was given to caressing and kissing gentlemen in the audience. Another of Fairlamb's spirit manifestations, a brazen, bearded man named George, liked to kiss women at séances, and his salty language sometimes scandalized listeners. Fairlamb and other female mediums thus became vessels for the spirits of men, allowing them to explore male language and even male embodiments in ways that, for some at least, proved liberating. More important, the direct connection that mediums established with the spirit world bypassed the male chain of command then characteristic of religious congregations.[3]

Women continue to be disproportionately represented in New Age religious practices. Regional magazines oriented to natural healing and alternative spirituality in New England typically advertise the services of roughly twice as many female practitioners as male, and the discrepancy is even greater if one limits the comparison to those who offer psychic counseling and psychotherapy. At channeling sessions, women often outnumber men by a factor of three to one or more, and the ratio of male to female channels is approximately 1:2 in New England and the Southwest.[4]

Channels typically account for this disparity by appealing to notions of inherent differences between the sexes. In a 1990 interview, Kim Westin and Ian Hanson, channels who provide spiritual counseling from the back of their bookstore in a former mining town in New Mexico, argued strongly that men and women have fundamentally different spiritual attributes and potentials. As we spoke, the corrugated iron roof of their store snapped and buckled under the blast-furnace sunlight of late June.

"Women are intuitive by nature," Ian mused.

Kim interrupted. "A woman is a natural receiver. A man is a natural sender."

"That's right," Ian agreed.

"For a man to be a trance medium or a channel, he has to be a feminine polarity in his male body to receive that information," Kim continued. "So there are far fewer feminine-polarity males than there are feminine-polarity or masculine-polarity females. But a masculine-polarity female isn't going to be a channel either. It's going to be a feminine-polarity or . . . "

Ian interjected, "It's all yin and yang. You've got it both, you know—the masculine and the feminine. And for me I'm . . . "

Kim ignored Ian's elaboration. "But it's the receiving types, not the outputting types, who are likely to be good channels," she said.

Ian persisted. "I can be yin or yang. I mean we *all* are, but it's easy for me to allow the feminine side to come in. A lot of men have subtle hang-ups when that sensitivity starts coming in. But I don't have any problems with that. I can get very yin, almost to the point where you'd say, 'Well, is the guy gay or what?' At the same time, though, I can turn that around and be aggressive and very, very yang."

Ian and Kim's animated burst of opinion about gender expresses beliefs held by many of those who are involved in channeling. Masculine and feminine represent two poles with contrasting attributes and predispositions. The masculine is rational, analytical, power-seeking, and self-absorbed; the feminine is emotional, intuitive, nurturing, and other-focused. About the root cause of these differences, however, there is considerable disagreement.

Some channels argue that the contrast between the sexes has been created by our upbringing. As one woman put it, "Women are trained to yearn for connections, while men are trained to yearn for individuality." Anna Swenson, the channel from upstate New York, put the issue more starkly: "Women haven't had the intuitive aspects beaten out of them." In a variation on this theme, some mentioned alleged developmental differences in the brain hemispheres of men and women. Social experience supposedly encourages men to favor left-brain activities (for instance, analytical thinking), whereas women are allowed to develop such right-brain functions as artistic creativity and holistic thinking.[5] Ironically, by discouraging women from involvement in politics and intellectual life, patriarchal oppression left them free to explore their intuitive powers. Because men were off playing power games, the argument goes, their own intuition withered.

Others contend that the differences between men and women begin at a deeper level, in genes or chromosomes or fundamental "energies" unique to each sex, forces that supposedly make women spiritual by nature. This view underlies Kim Westin's claim that women are natural receivers while men are natural senders. The female energy is perceived to be "more open to intuition, feelings, and emotions," whereas the male energy is seen to push men in the direction of analysis and self-consciousness. A channel from Massachusetts stressed women's skill in nonlinear thinking. "The act of channeling involves trust, intuition, and submission to a total experience. You have to be *in* it, not analyzing it at the same time," she said.

Such views echo nineteenth-century reasoning about why women were more likely than men to become mediums. Women, it was asserted then, are by nature impressionable, sentimental, passive, and even angelic—all qualities that open them to spiritual influence. Although today's female channels might object to the characterization of women as naturally passive, the rest of the portrait would strike them as accurate.

Another explanation offered for the predominance of women as channels is eschatological, based on the belief that history follows a sacred plan. Among those involved in women-centered spirituality, it is virtually an article of faith that all societies were once matriarchies dedicated to the worship of the Goddess. Matriarchal utopias, the story continues, were eventually overthrown by the male institutions that have dominated human history for the last three millennia. (The absence of support for this view among reputable scholars is considered further proof of patriarchal domination.) As our species moves toward a new synthesis of male and female, patriarchy is crumbling under the weight of its pathologies.

This eschatology has percolated into the worldview of channels and their clients. A New Mexico channel described recovered memories of her previous incarnations, dating to a period before the destruction of matriarchy. "I can remember lives of being in temples, and I can remember lives of being a medicine woman," she said. "I have memories of being empowered, of leading groups of people and communing with groups of women, doing Moon Lodges and all these wonderful things that are starting to happen again." For Sandy Randolph, also from New Mexico, the dark ages of male dominance were needed so that humans could understand the effects of imbalance. "There was a time for Spirit to withdraw and for people to have these experiences of competition and killing," she explained. "Spirit is now returning. You can see this in all the angels and entities that are coming through now." As this spiritual transition advances, women lead the way for men, many of whom are paralyzed by anxiety as their patriarchal world collapses around them.

Women's aptitude for intuitive work is cited to explain their over-representation at channeling events, as is the conviction that women can achieve a sense of accomplishment by developing their intuitive powers. Sandy Randolph, whose spiritual services include channeling and American Indian pipe ceremonies, argues that women predominate in her workshops because "it's time for them to give up their woundedness, to come back into their own feminine power." Occasionally, channels provide more prosaic reasons for the high proportion of women who turn out for workshops and lectures. With a mischievous grin, Jill Parsons, a channel from Santa Fe, claimed that single women also attend channeling events in hope of meeting a man who's "willing to open his heart and talk about what he feels," a quasi-mythical species of male known as a SNAG ("Sensitive New Age Guy").

Despite their celebration of the spiritual re-emergence of the feminine, most women involved in channeling distance themselves from feminism, which they describe as negative and reactive, a state of being against men. "I'm not a feminist, I'm a people-ist," one insisted, making clear her belief that gender should not be used to throw up walls between people. Pamela, a middle-aged channel from Santa Fe, put it this way: "Feminism is not equality to me. It's a response to male chauvinism that's taken to an extreme. I wouldn't be a feminist, but I'm an advocate of absolute equality between men and women." Like Pamela, most women involved in channeling hold feminist positions on grassroots issues: equal pay, child care, sex discrimination, and abortion rights. As a group, they are precisely the sort of self-confident, forceful women one might expect to identify with a feminist agenda. A contrast between strong support for the political goals of feminism and rejection of a feminist identity is hardly unique to channels; according to some feminist writers, it reflects a national pattern.[6] But what is particular to them as a group is their commitment to ideals of harmony and wholeness incompatible with what many see as feminism's confrontational outlook. Women involved in channeling seek an alliance between the sexes, not greater conflict. Some invoke the mystical integration of yin and yang to explain their search for balance between masculine and feminine powers. Others insist that sexual balance simply offers the best hope for happier lives. Such attitudes help to explain their enthusiastic defense of the men's movement, which finds few supporters among feminist intellectuals. The men's movement, among other things, claims to help men reconnect to the spirit of the primordial male at a time when male roles have become increasingly ambiguous. In explaining her sympathy for such experiments, one channel said, "The guys are having a hard time. There's no role model, no pattern for any kind of male energy now. That's why men's groups are wonderful."

Even the channels who identify themselves as committed feminists admit that channeling has made them more open to masculinity, if not to men. Katherine, a therapist who also holds a divinity degree, described how this transformation had taken place for her. "All the feminist stuff that we talked about in divinity school, that doesn't work for me anymore," she said, referring to feminism's focus on the coercive power of patriarchal institutions and attitudes. "In channeling, there isn't any agenda. There's no power in a negative sense." Katherine explained that one of her guardian spirits—a "gatekeeper," as she called him— is decidedly masculine, and their alliance has affected the way she looks at masculinity. "He's around a lot, and that relationship balances me in a way that gets me to understand masculine/feminine on a really experiential level." Katherine argues, in other words, that channeling offers direct experience of masculinity without the emotional risks associated with human relationships. For her, feminist theology is oriented to a "battle" between male and female, whereas her direct, channeled experience of masculinity is nonconfrontational. It heals the wounds of gender and allows her to move on to other things. Anita Sanderson, a close friend of Katherine's and a channel herself, agreed. "Channeling really has to do with balanced energetic forms of male and female. People are now coming to the place of exploring androgyny itself—not necessarily acting in a bisexual manner but simply holding balanced energy," she said.

Women who channel male spirits report that the experience has broadened their understanding of other ways of being. Deborah O'Neill explained her connection to the male entity Dwahl Khul in terms of a desire to offset her natural femininity: "A male guide provided an energy format that helped me to achieve male–female integration. At first I worried that I had a male, left-brained, scientific guide because of some patriarchal tendency on my part, but I found that the male was what I needed for greater integration." Deborah stressed that channeling provides a way to achieve totality by "filling in the gaps." For her, that means exploring masculine assertiveness in her spiritual work.

Some women disapprove of the predominance of male spirits that characterized channeling in the 1970s and 80s, attributing it to the lingering influence of patriarchy. Male figures, they observe, had more credibility in the channeling movement's initial stages. Tamara Jenkins, a Massachusetts channel who holds strongly feminist views, commented, "Many beginners channel male entities because they seem more authoritative. I warn people about this tendency in my channeling workshops." Sandy

Randolph sees her alliance with the Medicine Women, a group of Native American healers whom she regularly channels, as proof that the pattern is shifting. The spirits who contacted her "could have had many incarnations that were not female, yet they've chosen to represent themselves as female or feminine." For Sandy, their choice indicates a desire to "work with the matriarchy," thus helping to rebalance a world too long held in the grip of patriarchal control.

Male channels express views of gender similar to those of their female counterparts. They agree that the male domination of religion is ending, to everyone's benefit. Unlike women, who talk about their "opening to channel" as a process of discovering personal power, men tend to view it as a path to their feminine side: intuition, emotional availability, and a sense of connection to others. Nevertheless, a note of defensiveness sometime crept into men's descriptions of being male in a world undergoing spiritual feminization. A male channel in Florida spoke with approval of feminine empowerment but then added quickly that "Spirit can't be restricted solely to the feminine form." In New Mexico, a man talked of how much he had grown by learning to express his feelings openly, then confessed that he was "looking forward to the time when men don't feel like they have to make excuses for being male."

For male channels, channeling offers a forum for exploring alternatives to masculinity by allowing them to develop intuitive, poetic, or nurturing qualities that they associate with femininity. The balance or symmetry sought by women is seldom fully realized in men's channeling practice: there are few men who regularly channel female spirits, although some predicted that this will become more common as society moves toward gender balance. At present, however, most men consider the act of channeling to be feminizing enough in itself. James Borden, a channeling psychotherapist from New England, insisted at first that channeling had no effect on his gender identity. After reflecting a moment, however, he admitted that his experiences as a channel for feminine energies had broadened his understanding and enriched his spiritual life.

Gay channels disagree among themselves over whether their sexual orientation is a significant factor in their approach to channeling. Most feel that it is irrelevant, but Bryan Wood, a particularly outspoken New Mexico channel, alleged that many straight channels believe that gays and lesbians are spiritually unbalanced. "What they say is that gay people have a problem integrating their male and female energies, which I think is homophobic nonsense," he said. As a strategy for expanding his channeling practice, Bryan developed a less assertive form of counseling that would appeal to female clients uncomfortable with male authority figures. "There are a lot of feminists among my upper-class white clients," he explained. "I downgraded my authority so that I didn't offend them. I also came out about being gay. So feminists tend to be at ease with me because they see me as part of an oppressed group."

The search for internal gender balance, as well as the frequently stated desire for a new synergy of masculine and feminine principles in the world at large, has led channeling toward several versions of sacred androgyny, the notion that highly developed spiritual beings encompass male and female principles in fruitful complementarity. The prevailing belief in reincarnation provides conceptual support for such ideas. Channeling the entity Michael during a channeling session in Arizona, David Johnson explained that in different lifetimes individuals acquire experiences unique to each gender or sexual orientation. "About ten percent of the population on the planet is homosexual," David said, "because that's the percentage experiencing and needing to learn the lessons of homosexuality." Other necessary lessons can only be acquired through heterosexual experience, both as a man and as a woman, he explained. In the course of hundreds of reincarnations, in other words, we will inhabit bodies that live out all possible permutations of gender and sexuality. Our spiritual core incorporates all aspects of gender and therefore transcends them.

This line of thinking has given rise to a growing number of genderless spirits. Their channels describe them as citizens of different dimensions or galaxies that have either evolved past gender or never experienced it in the first place. From this vantage point, they analyze the sexual foibles of human beings and hold out the promise of a world in which these troubles can be eluded. An ardent follower of the teachings of Seth, the being channeled by Jane Roberts in the 1960s and 70s, mentioned Seth's assertion that humans are nothing but consciousness. "So there is no gender," she continued. "When you get back to what we really are outside of physical reality, there's no gender to any of us."

The healing power of androgyny is celebrated by a group of channels based in Sedona, Arizona, who claim to be walk-ins. In a video distributed by the group, which calls itself the Extraterrestrial Earth Mission, a man and two women dressed in matching yellow jumpsuits sit on a stage. The thickset man, who goes by the name of Aktivar, explains, "It is time for male/female balance to come to the fore. We talk to many beings about androgyny, which we find to be an exquisite state: delightful, balanced, beautiful, powerful!" The goal of Aktivar and his companions is to prepare us for the imminent metamorphosis of the planet, its transformation into a heavenly world of light. "Isn't it neat to be androgynous beings, because you get a fresh start! You get a chance to transcend all that bullshit that has developed over the ages." As he speaks, the woman to his left begins to channel high-pitched tones as her head wobbles in an erratic ellipse: "Whoooooo! Pah! Weeeeeep!" He seems unruffled by the sounds exploding from his companion. "By allowing your androgyny to come forth," he continues, "you are either in a male or female body, but you are not purely male or female. You are a third type."[7]

Another variation on the theme of androgyny was developed in a channeling session that took place in Santa Fe in the autumn of 1993. The advance literature for the event explained that a couple from Colorado were organizing meetings which would allow participants to "experience the empowering Love of the Divine Maternal-Paternal" by activating "the twelve-fold chakra system encoded within your DNA." The document implied that the event would expose participants to a channeled energy made up of strongly marked male and female qualities combined as a powerful, unitary force.

   The flier's allusion to something called the "I AM Presence" signaled that the channels' work was influenced by the "I AM" Religious Activity, founded in 1930 by a mining engineer named Guy Ballard and his wife, Edna. Ballard claimed to have experienced a series of revelations near Mt. Shasta, California. Appropriating names and concepts from Theosophy, Ballard reported a number of encounters with the Ascended Masters. Ballard explained that the Ascended Masters had evolved to the level of what he called the "I AM," the universal source of divinity. Prominent among them were Saint Germain (held by some to be an incarnation of Francis Bacon), his "twin flame" Portia, El Morya (once a Rajput priest), and Jesus Christ. Ballard assumed the role of messenger for the Ascended Masters, and he regularly delivered communiqués from Saint Germain and a host of lesser-known figures.

Writing under the name Godfre Ray King, Ballard described these visions in a series of books that became best-sellers. With the help of his wife and son, he organized a movement that by 1940 had attracted nearly a million followers. Ballard had a knack for making arcane teachings clear and accessible, and his books gave Theosophy an American face by locating the Ascended Masters in Mt. Shasta, Yellowstone, and the Tetons. After Ballard's death in 1939, the "I AM" Activity was torn by a series of internal disputes. Legal suits charging the "I AM" Activity with fraud were eventually overturned by the U.S. Supreme Court in two rulings (*Ballard v. United States,* 1944, and *Ballard v. United States,* 1946) now considered landmarks in the legal separation of church and state. By the 1950s, splinter elements within the "I AM" Activity had begun to make their own contacts with Ascended Masters, whose circle has widened to include extraterrestrials. Today many channels, some of whom know little about Guy Ballard and his work, claim to communicate with Ascended Masters, especially Saint Germain. Channels influenced by the "I AM" offer an erotically charged androgyny that differs markedly from the rather sexless androgyny offered by other practitioners.[8]

The leaders of the "I AM"-inspired event in Santa Fe were Diana and Alistair Lovejoy. Alistair, a spare, bearded man with unruly white hair, wore loose white cotton slacks and a blue polo shirt. He appeared to be in his sixties. The first thing one noticed about Diana was her diminutive size: she was well under five feet tall and needed to support her feet with a pillow to sit in a straight-backed chair. Her hair was light brown, running to blonde; crow's feet clustered around her eyes, breaking up the squareness of her features and lending an air of maturity to a face that otherwise looked younger than Alistair's. Diana was dressed in a beige-colored sweater, beige slacks, and white slippers.

The session took place in the home of Sarah McGuire and Ruth Como, practitioners of holistic healing and channeling. The living room decor of their adobe house was haute New Age: a beige rug, leather couches and chairs, candles, icons of spiritual masters, books hilled up on shelves. Gauzy autumn light, sifted through the leaves of a nearby cottonwood, fluttered on the wall. Soft music issued from a stereo in the far corner.

Counting Sarah, Ruth, and myself, six people had gathered in the living room with the Lovejoys. One was Mahmud, a gaunt but handsome Palestinian whose spiritual quest brought him to New Mexico, a place that reminded him of his home-land. Next was a young man named Jeff, who said that he was trying to resolve childhood issues and, like Mahmud, to arrive at a "heart-opening." The young woman on Mahmud's right, Theresa, identified herself as the assistant to a well-known Albuquerque channel. Later in the afternoon we were joined by Mark, a man from New England who had moved to Santa Fe as part of a personal religious search that had also taken him to California and Arizona. As the participants identified themselves and explained their motives for attending, Diana and Alistair listened attentively and radiated high-intensity friendliness.

While a signup sheet and a basket for donations (the suggested offering was $10) was passed around, Alistair explained that he and Diana had been together for five years. He had received instructions to seek out his "soul twin" at Mt. Shasta, the site where Guy Ballard had received his first messages from the Ascended Masters. As predicted, Alistair met Diana there, and they have been together ever since. Diana then took over the conversation. She converted to Mormonism in her late teens, she said, but the church excommunicated her when she began to channel Jesus, whom she called Yeshua Sananda. She eventually received the training necessary to channel the "I AM" energy in its multiple forms.

Alistair laid the philosophical groundwork for the session while Diana quietly sat next to him. He asked participants to open themselves so that the "I AM" energy could move in and through us. Diana's channeling would simply "mirror" us, he said, giving shape to the divine power surging through us all. Alistair began a long explanation of the "I AM" principles for the benefit of first-time participants. He named key Ascended Masters, including Saint Germain, Maitreya, Ashtar, and Kadar Mon-Ka, each of whom had a feminine counterpart. He explained that the rational mind has to give way to an emotional heart-opening based on unconditional love. We must become empty vessels for the transformative "I AM" energy, which we ourselves help to co-create. If we do this, the Divine Maternal will gently embrace all in her limitless love.

Alistair was in full tilt when Diana put her forefinger to his lips, quieting him. She sat up straight while Alistair adjusted a tape recorder. After a long invocation, Diana closed her eyes and breathed deeply. Minutes passed. She opened her eyes and began to speak in a gently accented voice, a warm, reassuring alto. (It was, Alistair told us later, the presence of Master Saint Germain.) Smiling beatifically, Diana called us "beloveds" and "dear ones." Her words flowed poetically, ranging out across the universe and then circling back to people in the room. "I assure you," she said, "that while at times it seems as though the Father–Mother and that radiant being called Christ might appear to be behind a closed door, in truth that door is always open. And the Father–Mother have stepped beyond the threshold and entered upon the path and run out to meet you." During a pause in the monologue, Alistair quietly interjected, "We receive your limitless love in our hearts with profound gratitude for this reflection of who we are."

After carrying on as Saint Germain for ten minutes, Diana again began to breathe deeply. She emerged from this state to ask Alistair for help: he should bring her a container of rose oil from an adjoining room. "Dear hearts," she told us in her mellifluous voice, "I request your permission to enter more profoundly into your energy field, to come to each of you." She added that if we did not want her to come into our sacred field, she would honor our wishes. Alistair explained that our energy had called forth "the I AM presence of Yeshua Sananda and his divine complement, Mary Magdalena, blended in a perfect balance of masculine and feminine." This, he continued, would summon "the divine maternal energies of unconditional love to bless us." The Yeshua–Magdalena presence is a sacred gift, he said.

Diana sang a simple song—several notes, deep and sustained. The words were indecipherable. Turning to Sarah, she commenced a ceremony that was part blessing, part anointing. She stood over Sarah with her right hand raised, two fingers pointing up. Her breath came with a rasping sound. She asked permission to come into Sarah's space. Diana rubbed rose oil on her own hand and then made slow circles in the air around Sarah's head. She slowly closed in on Sarah's face: touching her forehead, her temples, her throat. She gently brought Sarah's hand up to touch her own chest above the heart. Diana began to sing again; the words sounded vaguely like Hebrew. This time, the song was nearly a howl, abrasive and unsettling in the absolute quiet of the room. Diana knelt before Sarah and took her left hand, rubbed oil onto it, slowly touched the palm in various places, then gently kissed the palm. She repeated the process with the right. She moved to Sarah's feet, carefully rubbing each with rose oil. Diana's breath still rasped loudly. She stood before Sarah, looking into her eyes. The words they exchanged were inaudible. The process was excruciatingly long, perhaps fifteen minutes. Her movements were gentle but labored. Tears welled up in Sarah's eyes.

Moving around the room, Diana repeated the procedure with the others, although the details varied slightly with each. Alistair occasionally explained what was happening. "Know that Diana isn't representing Mary Magdalena," he said at one point. "Mary has presented herself in Diana through the divine energy of I AM, the I AM Presence in all of us. The maternal force of Mary Magdalena is coupled with the twin-flame masculine presence of Yeshua Sananda, whom you know as Jesus." The implication seemed to be that the integration of Jesus and Mary Magdalena generated a sexual synergy that was far more powerful than masculine or feminine energies alone.

After performing the ritual with everyone, Diana returned to her chair. The process had taken an hour and a half. Mary Magdalena–Yeshua Sananda wished everyone well and departed. Diana became her normal self moments later. Diana rubbed her eyes during the long silence that followed. Alistair was the first to speak. "This is amazing," he said. "You must know how honored you are. This is only the third time that the Magdalena–Yeshua presence has manifested in Diana. You have been bathed in the nurturing warmth of the Mother Energy." People began to exchange impressions, sharing the emotions they had experienced while Diana worked on them. As we gathered our things to leave, Alistair urged us to drink plenty of distilled water with lemon. Otherwise, he said, we would feel exhausted because of all the energy that had flowed through our bodies during the event.

Diana Lovejoy's erotically charged language, with its "twin flames" and "empowering Love of the Divine Maternal–Paternal," defines a world in which the combination of male and female energy produces a spiritual incandescence that burns with the intensity of nuclear fusion. More typical of contemporary channeling, however, is a relatively sexless androgyny, the performance of which establishes for both practitioner and audience that the human soul exists at a level beyond such earthly considerations as gender, with all its dilemmas and limitations.

The gender play characteristic of contemporary American channeling is found among spirit mediums in other parts of the world. In Africa, Latin America, and Asia, women are more likely than men to be possessed by spirits, many of whom are identified as male. The reasons for this are fairly straightforward. Women are often excluded from formal positions of religious power, so they fight for a voice in religious matters by speaking for capricious spirits whose opinions men are obliged to respect.

A vivid example of how women use spirits to overcome powerlessness is provided by Michael Lambek, a Canadian anthropologist who for the past twenty years has studied spirit possession on Mayotte, an island lying off the southeastern coast of Africa. In one case of possession documented by Lambek, two women entered trance simultaneously. Their spirits began a conversation that focused on conflicts between one of the women and her husband. The woman's spirit spoke forthrightly of her objections to his drinking and other personal failings. The husband, who was present during the event, then had to defend himself publicly against the spirit's accusations. This exchange can be seen as a form of family therapy in which the woman and her husband use spirits to mediate a discussion of problems that are too sensitive to be talked about directly. The work of Lambek and others has made it virtually a cliché that spirit possession represents women's resistance to the overweening power of men.[9] But is this true for channels in the United States as well?

There is no simple answer. Like other useful terms that find their way into academic fashion, "resistance" has been reduced to a platitude nearly stripped of meaning. Nevertheless, there is little doubt that women are drawn to contemporary channeling for the same reasons that they were a strong presence in nineteenth-century spiritualism—notably, their continued exclusion from positions of influence in mainstream churches. In that sense, women who channel may be resisting male power or claiming it for themselves. But with few exceptions, channels themselves reject this way of looking at it. Instead, they see their quest in proactive terms, as a positive, loving search for personal strength and global healing between the sexes.

It is important to remember that channeling is only one element of a much larger mosaic of religious options open to Americans. Other pieces of the mosaic offer forums in which women can work through rage or confusion over the injuries of gender. An anthropologist who worked closely with neopagan groups, some of which promote a militantly feminist spirituality, found that they celebrate what she calls "images of anger and destruc-

tion." For women involved in neopagan worship, this dark imagery can be therapeutic.[10] Channeling, in contrast, offers safe
haven from such emotions. In its embrace, men and women can
explore the qualities of the opposite sex as part of a journey of
self-expansion that leaves a gendered identity far behind, a process that female channels in particular find satisfying.[11]

But do such performances reshape conventional sex roles in
significant ways? Current theories of gender suggest that they
might. Scholars have proposed that gender is less a fixed condition—something hard-wired into our genes—than it is a state of
mind and body maintained through daily performance. Movements, gestures, dress codes, and subtle inflections of voice constitute the raw materials of gender display. What performances
create, they can also undo, subtly shifting the boundaries of gendered identities. Women who channel claim direct experience
of pure masculinity—"clear male energy," as one put it—that
dramatically broadens their understanding and, in their view,
strengthens their sense of personal power. They encounter this
male energy in a physical, embodied way. They *enact* masculinity, in other words, which may help them to domesticate it or
otherwise render it less threatening. The gender enactments of
male channels are not yet symmetrical to those of women, for
few are inclined to embody feminine beings. Many seem to be
moving in that direction, though, and most cultivate a slightly
androgynous style in their self-presentation. For men, it may be
feminizing enough to relinquish control to the outside force of
spirits. Whether experienced directly or merely witnessed by
members of an audience, ritual performances of androgyny have
the effect of making gender seem, to quote the anthropologist
Janice Boddy, "less naturalized, less unquestionable, indeed, less
subjectively real."[12]

Paradoxically, this gender play depends on the acceptance of a highly polarized view of masculinity and femininity—for instance, the belief that men are by nature rational, women intuitive, and so forth. For channels and their clients, however, these absolute, "natural" states are not models to which they aspire; instead, they are envisioned as diffuse energies that can be interwoven and rebalanced to suit personal needs. Like so much of the bricolage or creative blending that characterizes New Age spirituality, the gender work that takes place in channeling is oriented to an amplification of the self. During her channeling workshop in Santa Fe, Deborah O'Neill explained to participants that when a man channels, he connects to something "poetic and creative and softer." For a woman, in contrast, channeling offers the experience of "taking authority and standing in a seemingly masculine position." Above all, channeling offers both men and women the opportunity to "feel and act as if all your gaps had been filled." "When you're channeling," she concluded, "you're asking for your totality."

6

DREAMING OF COMMUNITY

Events that bring people together to celebrate their collective identity—feasts, barn-raisings, weddings, funerals—may create a whole greater than the sum of the parts, an order beyond the personal. As social beings, humans can be invigorated or destroyed by the collective energy of the group. Even channels, most of whom are committed to an intensely individualistic form of spirituality that shuns orthodoxy and compromise, must occasionally come together to share experiences and to taste what Emile Durkheim, one of the founders of sociology, referred to as the "effervescence" of communal worship. Many, in fact, insist that their work is laying the foundation for a global renaissance of community. Adam Bell, a New Mexico channel, explained that the spirits to whom he connects speak frequently of the need for humanity to join together in cooperative ventures. "Community is a common theme among the entities," he said. Deborah O'Neill echoed Adam's comments when she declared that channeling helps her "to become less identified with our culture, our sex, and our race, and more identified with the universal sense of human nature."

The tension between the private experience of channeling and the desire to obtain support from others confronts channels and their clients with a series of perplexing questions. What social arrangements, for example, offer the optimal balance of freedom and fellowship? Is it possible to translate a deeply felt commitment to global community into civic involvement at the local level, and if so, how? The answers to such questions reveal changes in American religious attitudes that extend far beyond channeling and the New Age movement.

One thing that the vast majority of channels clearly do not associate with community is anything that resembles a formal religion, with regular meetings and a stable organizational structure. For them, and for most of those drawn to New Age practices, the term "religion" is freighted with negative meanings: empty rituals, inflexible rules, and struggles for power. These stand opposed to spirituality, "the process of connecting with all that is inside," to quote one channel's formulation.[1]

Objections to religion cluster around several themes. "Conventional religions," one woman insisted, "have too much doctrine, too much 'if you don't do it this way then you're going to hell.'" Diane, a channel from western Massachusetts, framed the issue this way: "My personal feeling is that when you keep questioning, keep growing, there comes a point where you'll be up against the outer limits of any religion. At that moment, the religion says, 'That's it, no more questioning.'" Another woman argued that established religions offer no space for creativity: "I don't fit into organized religion at any level, so it would be a waste of my energy to try. I like the creative aspect of a disorganized movement like channeling. It's better for an artistic temperament."

Not only do religions fail to offer authentic spirituality, channels argue, they are obsolete vestiges of an earlier historical era. "Churches are old-fashioned in their paradigm," one explained. They may have served a useful role by creating a sense of belonging or, as one man suggested, by imposing taboos to protect people from unhealthy food, but these functions have long since outlived their purpose. Most people concede that the world's major religions began with a genuine spiritual core, but in their view this was eventually corrupted by power. Ted Bernstein, a channel from Arizona, dismissed religion with this well-practiced slogan: "Religions are spiritual movements that stopped moving."

From the perspective of people attracted to channeling and similar forms of improvisational spirituality, the major problem with formal religions is their alleged obsession with hierarchy and control. Susan, a woman attending a channeling session in New Mexico, expressed this idea in the starkest possible terms. "All religions were founded out of a desire to control people or to keep a group of people subservient," she said. "Every religion I've ever studied or known about evolved into one group controlling another." Evidence of this hierarchical imperative is found in the exclusion of women from positions of power. For Rebecca, a Massachusetts channel and self-identified feminist, the choice is clear: "The major religions are based on the exclusion of women. Channeling isn't organized—it has no group aspect—so women have a better position in it." Such negative views are challenged by a few who speak fondly of the religious traditions of their upbringing, yet even these apologists admit that their experience of religion lacked spiritual depth. "I was raised in a middle-class, Jewish family," one woman explained. "But I was given more tradition than religion. We did all the traditional things. But no one ever explained it from a spiritual point of view. It was tradition without a strong spiritual component."

Several channels mentioned that they had joined an organized congregation for a while, often the Unitarian Church or the Church of Religious Science. They justified their choice in purely pragmatic terms—a desire to expose their children to organized worship, perhaps, or their need for a reliable support group. Usually they left the congregation after a year or two because they had "outgrown" its theology or decided that it was time to "get more deeply into my own issues." Like other therapeutic resources, church allegiance shifted as their needs evolved.

New Age complaints about mainstream churches echo with remarkable fidelity the protests of spiritualists in the 1850s. Spiritualist magazines of the period railed against the "dead formalism" of Christianity. Spiritualism encouraged people to consider all religious ideas, as a result of which they were "receiving and practicing the profoundest and holiest truths."[2] Nineteenth-century critics of mainstream churches were more preoccupied with the churches' wealth than are their counterparts today, and their rhetoric was far more likely to emphasize the link between spiritualism and true Christianity. But today's channels share with yesterday's spiritualists the belief that American freedoms include the right, perhaps even the duty, to pursue growth beyond the arbitrary limits set by institutions.

If churches are incompatible with personal growth, how do those involved in channeling come together for mutual support? The two most important models of fellowship that have emerged since the 1970s are the informal self-help group, in which several people agree to form a temporary alliance, and the professional counseling session or group workshop, in which a channel provides information to clients for a fee.

Stories about self-help groups permeate the life histories of people involved in channeling. Take the case of Mary Selmer, a 45-year-old housewife from western New England. Some years ago, she began to meet regularly with friends to listen to audio tapes made by J. Z. Knight. Mary described her circle of seekers as a bunch of "beer-drinking and cigarette-smoking New Agers" who sat for hours on her porch discussing metaphysical questions. They experimented with group meditation, and during one session, Jim, a chiropractor by training, began to channel spontaneously. At first the words were slow and indistinct, Mary said, "but stuff was definitely coming through." As Jim became more adept at channeling, the group met weekly to interview his spirits. After a few months, however, the meetings lost momentum. "What happened is that we ran out of questions as a group," she said. "We needed new faces." The circle disbanded, and Jim went on to establish a successful channeling practice in a neighboring state.

Informal channeling groups are, almost by definition, ephemeral and private. Channeling's public face is the lecture or workshop that lasts from several hours to a week or more. When channels appear in public, their goal is to share information provided by spirit entities. Some also believe that their contact with spirits bathes the audience in healing energies. Several admitted that they like to give public lectures because the broad, philosophical content of the talks is a refreshing change from the sometimes tedious work of helping clients wrestle with personal problems. The lectures have a pragmatic goal as well: to give potential clients a sense of a channel's style, possibly leading to a request for private counseling.

In June 1990 a typical channeling session took place in the house of Bryan Wood, who has a lively practice as a psychic and spiritual teacher in New Mexico. Bryan channels the Clan, which his résumé describes as a "non-hierarchical, non-authoritarian, genderless information source." This meeting was the last of a series during which the Clan elaborated a scheme for understanding the spiritual dimensions of the human personality. At the session were nineteen people—twelve women and seven men—most of whom were older than 30. They chatted quietly and arranged themselves around the living room on couches and pillows. Those who had attended the previous classes knew each other well, but about half of the group appeared to be new to Bryan's circle.

Pulling up a straight-backed chair, Bryan called the group to order. A stocky man with long graying hair, Bryan is articulate, broadly educated, and flamboyantly opinionated, the latter trait contrasting sharply with the nonjudgmental quality of most channels. For the occasion, he held a tape recorder in one hand and in the other a fist-sized rock. After a few announcements, Bryan closed his eyes. His head jerked sharply to the left, and he sighed deeply. Thirty seconds later, he began to speak as the Clan. His voice was pitched slightly higher than usual; his diction became formal and precise. (As a handout distributed by Bryan explained: "The Clan projects no personality. It's not very entertaining. It has identified itself as a group of energies focused on various levels of reality.") Except for occasional movements of his head, Bryan's body was immobile throughout the session.

In its droning voice, the Clan outlined the subject of discussion: "And we welcome you this evening. Understand that our topic for discussion is the utopian neighborhood and how it can be created in reality given your present limitations and mindset. The entire purpose for this series of lectures has been to bring through metaphysical, spiritual, intellectual, and emotional tools for individual humans to tap into their divinity so that peace is possible, not only on a global level but on the local level and personal level from which the global level springs as a mirror."

For the next fifty minutes, the Clan, through Bryan, developed ideas about the establishment of perfect communities. First it was asserted that the world can only be improved by working on ourselves. All humans are divine beings—"autonomous, self-directive, immortal, and perfect," in the words of the Clan—but we must discover our true passions in order to focus personal energies in constructive ways. Bad things happen in the world because people try to change others rather than themselves. To create a utopian neighborhood, in other words, we must first take responsibility for our own happiness. Throughout the lecture, the people in the room seemed relaxed and attentive. One woman sat with eyes closed, devoutly holding a green crystal.

Eventually Bryan rubbed his face, marking his exit from trance. He put down the tape recorder to announce a short break. The visitors stretched and stepped outside in the hope of catching a breeze, for the small room had grown close in the evening heat. Someone passed around pieces of melon. After ten minutes, Bryan called everyone back into the room and quickly reentered trance. The Clan invited questions. Those who had attended earlier classes asked for clarification on various points—philosophical issues, terminological matters, and so forth. An hour later, the session came to a close. "We will simply leave you with this thought," the Clan said. "You have the power to change the world, to be precisely the world you want. But it will not come through trying to change others. It will come from saying yes to your situation, then from the decision, moment by moment, to give yourself unconditional love."

After coming out of trance, Bryan invited us to stay as long as we liked. He mentioned that audio tapes of previous sessions could be purchased for $10 each and that he and the Clan were available for personal counseling. A donation of $5 was welcome for this session, he added, but by no means required.

It is not easy to establish intimacy at public channeling events, for those who attend are likely to be complete strangers. Bryan solved this problem by organizing a lecture series, during which some of the participants came to know one another fairly well. Other channels may lack a clientele large enough to sustain more than an occasional public lecture. To break the ice in small gatherings, channels often ask participants to introduce themselves and talk about their reasons for attending. Invitations to form a hand-holding circle also foster a sense of shared experience. Intimacy presents its own problems, though. During question-and-answer sessions, one client may doggedly pursue personal issues to the point that others, anxious to move on to broader themes, become restless. Experienced channels ease the discussion back to philosophical matters or tactfully convince the questioner to leave the issue for private counseling.

At most channeling sessions, the prevailing emotional tone is similar to that of the event at Bryan's house: philosophical, gently humorous, and relatively impersonal. This is surprising in light of the widespread belief that people experiment with new religions as part of a search for emotional catharsis. Channels themselves frequently talk about the importance of connecting to their clients' emotional and physical centers rather than to their intellects. Yet channeling sessions also suggest an intellectual hunger as well, a desire to explore complex philosophical issues such as the nature of time and the links between the spiritual and physical worlds. There are, of course, exceptions. Events that include guided meditations are more likely to evoke collective sighs of contentment or tears of happiness. Nevertheless, compared to the intensely emotional self-help workshops and support-group meetings taking place across the nation today, most channeling sessions are reserved and meditative affairs.

From the point of view of participants, workshops and channeled lectures offer an ideal balance of group engagement and individual autonomy. The level of personal commitment is low, and one need attend only as often as seems rewarding. Although the channel directs the events that take place in a workshop, the hierarchy implicit to the situation is only temporary. The nature of the "community" generated by encounters such as this follows the pattern articulated by Bryan Wood's channeled entities, the Clan: the group mirrors the personal development of those who constitute it. In other words, if the individual participants find the event fulfilling, then their mutual growth transforms the group into an ideal microcosm of community.

The attitudes of channels and their clients toward established churches, and to society as a whole, reveal a deep mistrust of structure, which they see as inherently hostile to personal growth and to an awareness of the sacred. Most channels proved skeptical even of utopian communes that try to integrate sacred principles into everyday life. The comments of a woman who spent several years in a spiritual community in Maine were typical: "There's always some kind of stuff to deal with in spiritual communities. It's hard to develop your own identity. There's usually some kind of leader, and you end up with a system that everyone's supposed to follow. I finally gave up that path because I wanted to connect to my own source of spirit." Although New Age settlements such as the Findhorn Community in Scotland and Sparrow Hawk Village in Oklahoma are important symbols of the dawning of a new era, they attract only a tiny fraction of people interested in channeling and related spiritual practices.[3]

Wariness of conventional communities sometimes verges on nihilism. Channels often assert that government on all levels is so morally bankrupt that it might as well be abandoned. Mimi Atkinson-Jones, whose book of channeled insight was published by a major commercial press, insisted that without inner healing, the processes of making and sustaining a community are hopelessly flawed. "All you need to do is go to some city council meetings," she observed. "What you see there is the projection of people's fear and inadequacy. We have to have inner communication to figure out who we are first, then those communities that we want can really happen." Others insist that they are passionately committed to the idea of community—but a universal community, not a local, sectarian one. "Look," one channel said, "we are really trying to become global citizens." In this view, the local becomes intrinsically parochial and negative, whereas a global perspective offers a high enough level of abstraction to transcend petty interests based on race, class, or nationality.

This vision of global community converges in unexpected ways with rhetoric about the world-wide network of cables and computers formally known as the Internet. Channeling's key metaphor, connection to the universal All-That-Is, finds a perfect match in the utopian language of the Internet's many poets, who celebrate its role in "wiring human and artificial minds into one planetary soul."[4] Observations such as this lead to the belief, shared by many in the overlapping worlds of New Age thought and computer-mediated communication, that the Internet is the first step toward communion with universal mind.

The problem with Internet-based community, however, is that it is both specialized and diluted. "Probably the first thing anybody notices when they go online," writes another believer in the Net's social magic, "is the community-building taking place all through cyberspace. Old people talk to old people, lonely gay teens find other lonely gay teens . . . truckers chat with truckers."[5] Here community consists of a shared identity rather than an enduring commitment to a circle of neighbors and kin. From the New Age perspective, electronic communications provide a perfect way to apply the Hundredth Monkey principle by creating a critical mass of people whose collective thought will change the world. Unanswered is the question of how the new global village will build schools, repair streets, collect garbage, and keep the peace. Although the sense of togetherness fostered by the Net seems only like ersatz community to anyone who has spent time in a peasant village, it is deeply felt by many of those who experience it. The profound sense of connection offered by the new technology leads users to see spiritual power in the Net itself. Self-described cybershamans propose that the Net's virtual space can be manipulated much as a tribal shaman controls the visionary space of trance. Participants in one online discussion group that I tracked for about a year even proposed that the Net could serve as an electronic Ouija board that would allow them to reestablish contact with the entity Seth.

The odd convergence between New Age thought and the experience of connection offered by the Internet reflects a distrust of institutions and ideologies that seems to be intensifying as our society becomes more complex. By limiting interpersonal contacts to those who share identical interests and goals, New Age workshops and Internet discussion groups create a sense of connection, of virtual community, that is often experienced far more vividly than the increasingly ambiguous and conflicted relations typical of the everyday world. As Sherry Turkle observes in her book *Life on the Screen,* the participants in multi-user domains (MUDs), computer discussion groups in which participants take on new identities and invent entire social worlds, often report that they like the safe virtual streets and safe virtual sex better than the real thing. "MUD friendships are more intense than real ones, and when things don't work out you can always leave," Turkle notes.[6] Like their counterparts on the Internet, people drawn to channeling experience the sense of togetherness achieved in workshops—a collective consciousness based entirely on temporary, elective participation in a small-group process—as more authentic than conventional civic activity in their neighborhoods and towns.

Despite the diffuse and sporadic group activities that characterize the work of most channels, many Americans associate channeling with cults, mostly because of a few highly publicized groups led by charismatic channels. J. Z. Knight is sometimes identified as a cult leader because she has gathered a loose-knit group of clients and supporters near her estate in Yelm, Washington. Far more controversial is Elizabeth Clare Prophet, known to her followers as Guru Ma, who heads the Church Universal and Triumphant. Prophet inherited the title of Messenger of the Great White Brotherhood from her husband, Mark Prophet, after his death in 1973. Two decades earlier, he had formed a splinter group of the "I AM" Activity that gradually evolved into the

Church Universal and Triumphant (CUT). Elizabeth Prophet continues to channel information from Saint Germain and other Ascended Masters as her primary source of revelation. In contrast to most New Age practice, however, CUT's principles are authoritarian and puritanical.

CUT became the focus of intense journalistic interest in the late 1980s when Prophet moved the church from California to a 12,000-acre ranch in Corwin Springs, Montana, adjacent to Yellowstone National Park. Acting on revelations that a nuclear Armageddon would take place in 1990, Prophet organized the construction of a massive underground complex designed to accommodate the estimated two thousand followers who relocated to the ranch and surrounding communities. The date on which Prophet had predicted nuclear disaster passed without incident, but stories that CUT was warehousing assault rifles, armored personnel carriers, and cases of ammunition on church property alarmed law-enforcement officials and led to the indictment of Prophet's husband, Edward Francis, on charges of using false names to acquire firearms. Local concern grew dramatically in 1993 after the violent confrontation between the federal government and Branch Davidians in Texas. Eventually, federal authorities and CUT leaders entered into a series of negotiations that led to the voluntary removal of arms from CUT property in exchange for partial restoration of the group's tax-exempt status. Today CUT continues to operate from its Montana headquarters and small local branches scattered around the nation and abroad.[7]

Peter Goldman, a compact man in his early forties with intense blue eyes, describes himself as a "cult survivor" who for five years was deeply involved in the Church Universal and Triumphant's activities in California, prior to the group's relocation to Montana. In his twenties, Peter investigated various religious movements in search of a message that would give meaning to his life. When he attended a CUT conference in California, he met many young men like himself, leading him to conclude that the movement was right for him. He was especially impressed by Elizabeth Prophet's dramatic channeling sessions. "She's very powerful, very hypnotic, very charismatic," he said. Before Prophet's public channeling sessions, the audience would engage in several hours of "decreeing," a form of chanting that Prophet insisted could literally change the world. "She'll have people decreeing for hours, and then she'll come onto the platform. By then you're in a trance and ready for an imprint. So she comes out looking like the Messenger and talking like the Messenger and having followers like the Messenger. So you think that she's the Messenger." Peter was drawn to Prophet in part because she was a woman. "I was a feminist even then," he said. "I thought, 'Great, a woman leader, the Divine Mother, the feminine aspect of God.'"

After moving to the CUT campus, Peter found himself drawn into an exhausting cycle of work, study, and decreeing. Eventually he concluded that decreeing and other techniques used by CUT were designed to make people psychologically malleable. Peter described an incident in which Prophet rebuked him severely for simply greeting her; she then sent him a note explaining that the reprimand had come from a spirit who wanted to put him into "alignment." Today he sees alignment as a code-word for "breaking me, breaking my spirit, my sense of self." After several years, he could no longer ignore CUT practices that offended him, including the obligatory chanting of negative decrees against apostate former members of the church. Peter abandoned CUT and found employment in a series of sales jobs. Today he and some friends edit a small-circulation magazine that promotes a positive attitude through the use of humor.

Despite his disillusionment with Elizabeth Clare Prophet and her church, Peter still believes that some channels have important, truthful messages to convey. He lavished praise on the teachings of Lazaris, the entity channeled by Jach Pursel, one of the most successful mediums in the country. But Peter described himself as wary of spiritual communities, especially those that embrace poverty. "It's an excuse for not making it," he said. "You can be poor if you want, but it's just not practical." For Peter, practicality is the ultimate test of spirituality: "Human transcendence is nice, but if it's not making your life better, if it's not making you happier, more free to do what you really want to do, more free of compulsions and neurosis or whatever—then it's not worth doing."

Susan Landry, a 34-year-old health-care worker living in upstate New York, described her experiences in another cult-like community organized by a charismatic channel. The channel, whom I'll call Richard Fletcher, was part New Age guru, part New York hustler, yet someone with an intuitive grasp of human character and an ability to channel strikingly accurate information. With funds provided by a wealthy disciple, Fletcher bought an abandoned summer camp that he planned to turn into a school for spiritual studies. Susan and about thirty of Fletcher's followers purchased homes and small businesses nearby. Susan was profoundly moved by the teachings of Kumar, the extraterrestrial being that Fletcher regularly channeled. "After meeting Kumar," she recalls, "the skies opened for me. Kumar said that everything was a seed that will manifest at some time and on some level, even if it doesn't manifest physically. So it's our responsibility to plant good seeds."

Fletcher's circle of clients continued to grow, but the school failed to develop as Susan and her friends had dreamed. His behavior became increasingly erratic, perhaps because of the responsibility of guiding so many people. "I think that his role got too big for him," she said. Eventually the community collapsed, and its members spun off in new directions. Despite this failure, Susan looks back on the experiment with as much affection as disappointment. She holds fond memories of the group's energy and idealism, the sense of building something important. Things went sour in the end, but for her "it was the major schooling of my lifetime." If there was a mistake, it was in yielding control to a single teacher. Susan concluded her story by quoting the words of a Sufi sage: "The best teacher to have is a dead one."

On close inspection, channeling proves largely peripheral to the use of power in the two groups with which Susan and Peter were involved. Like the happy families in Tolstoy's famous dictum, authoritarian sects are all the same. Under the watchful eye of a charismatic leader, believers cut their ties to friends and kin, the reference-points of their prior lives. The group substitutes a new map, redefining the terrain of belief and turning disciples into social children exquisitely sensitive to praise or reproach.

Channeling, however, has a democratic undercurrent that subverts centralized power. Peter Goldman, the ex-CUT member, reported that CUT persecuted anyone else in the church who claimed contacts with spirits, denouncing them as "false hierarchy impostors." This is ironic in view of the fact that the founder of CUT, Mark Prophet, had broken away from the "I AM" Activity so that he could become a Messenger of the Ascended Masters over the objections of the group's leadership, which claimed monopolistic control over channeled information. The subversively democratic quality of channeling can be seen in the history of other movements as well. In the Oneida Community of the nineteenth century, the leadership of John Humphrey Noyes was undermined by the involvement of community members in spiritualism, which provided them with information that sometimes contradicted Noyes's prophetic visions.[8]

Most people involved in channeling are reluctant to express judgments about cult-like groups such as CUT. In response to a question about authoritarian gurus, a Florida man said, "Well, guru is spelled G-U-R-U. You know, 'Gee, you are you.'" By this he meant that people find powerful teachers as part of their process of growth, even though this might produce transitional dependency. Pamela, a New Mexico channel who earlier in life had suffered under the reign of authoritarian spiritual teachers, put it this way: "They weren't right for me, but they were right for others. People go where they need to go to get what they need to get." A common New Age observation about cults is that those who fall into them are "fulfilling certain lessons" related to their spiritual evolution. Nevertheless, most channels are quick to distance themselves from what they see as the pathological power dynamics of authoritarian groups.

On balance, channeling as practiced in the United States today, defined as it is by individualism and radical relativism, offers a weak foundation for tightly-knit charismatic organizations. By nature, cults depend on rigorous boundary control, something that is hard to reconcile with channeling.[9] Even if a charismatic leader claims direct access to powerful spirits, there is little to keep someone else from contacting the same beings. A visit to any New Age bookstore reveals that the arena of channeled entities is today so crowded that none can establish a monopoly on cosmic truth. As if designed by Adam Smith, channeling offers a world of perfect competition.

Although the inherently centrifugal teachings of channeling provide a weak foundation for communities of worship, some groups manage to overcome these tendencies and achieve a degree of stability. To understand how New Age ideas might be integrated into conventional religious life, I attended the weekly services of two congregations that make use of channeling and related New Age practices.[10]

Once a month, the Archangel Gabriel holds forth in the Temple of Light Ascendant, a modest shingled chapel in upstate New York. The archangel's channel, and the pastor of the Temple of Light Ascendant, is the Reverend Sally McIntire, who founded the church thirty years ago. In keeping with its mission as a Christian metaphysical church, the Temple's weekly services count on the participation of several mediums from within the congregation, who share inspirational messages from the spirit world. But when the Archangel Gabriel takes center stage, the services attract a hundred people or more, about three times the average Sunday attendance.[11]

On a sultry August night in 1993, ceiling fans churned the warm air as people filed into the sanctuary. Elderly women in polyester dresses sat next to young men with ponytails. There was a scattering of Asian, African-American, and Hispanic faces. Friends hugged each other and chatted happily as people streamed in through the front door.

At the appointed hour, the Reverend Sally took a seat in the chancel. A snowy-haired woman who appeared to be in her fifties, she wore slacks and a blouse as white as her hair. From her neck dangled a small crystal on a chain. After a young Asian-

American woman welcomed the congregation, the floor was turned over to a man with a guitar, who led a rendition of "A Closer Walk with Thee." Before beginning the song, he announced a change of lyrics: rather than "I am weak but thou art strong," he invited the congregation to sing "I am light and thou art strong." This was the first of several impromptu revisions that removed all references to weakness, guilt, or inadequacy from traditional hymns. After a recitation of the Metaphysician's Creed, which asserts belief "in the continuity of Life proved by communication with those in the spirit realm," the lights were lowered for a meditation. The meditation leader encouraged people to let go of their concerns about personal limitations or failings. "We are perfect; we are God," she said. "We are reaching for the highest part of ourselves, the highest good, the most perfect acceptance of ourselves." There were sighs of happiness throughout the room.

Sally McIntire rose to the podium and greeted the gathering in the persona of the Archangel Gabriel. Gabriel's words were spiced by an accent reminiscent of New Delhi or Bombay, and his sentences sometimes tumbled over themselves as if English were not his first tongue. When late arrivals clustered near the temple's front door, for instance, Gabriel pointed toward empty seats in the front and said, "There are some places to put your body in a sitting position. Come forth." As in the speech of other channels, however, colloquialisms elbowed their way into this flow of odd constructions, to the delight of the congregation. As Gabriel spoke, the Reverend Sally looked around the room and moved her arms expressively. Occasionally she sipped juice from a glass on the podium. There was a surprising lightness to the atmosphere.

Gabriel's sermon touched on points made earlier in the service. Everyone can achieve perfection, limitlessness, and completeness, he said. Illness and death are illusions that we create for ourselves. If we embrace the idea of old age and death, Gabriel insisted, we trick the body into believing in their reality: "You can live your life in total freedom from limitations. There is nothing that is greater than *you*. Nothing. Go forth and be whatever you want. But don't track mud on the clouds!" The upbeat news transmitted by Gabriel, which at points was delivered with an almost rhythmic insistence, is typical of the kind of statement known as an "affirmation"—that is, a declaration believed to bring about a desired outcome through repeated performance. Affirmations are rooted in the New Thought movement of the nineteenth century, which asserted the power of positive thinking to heal illness and create prosperity.[12]

After the collection and another song, the Reverend Sally invited questions for the Archangel. With little hesitation, people came forward to a microphone. Addressing the pastor as Gabriel, a white woman asked whether there were other groups receiving these teachings. Gabriel replied that such groups exist in France, Australia, and Canada. "But why should you be in contact with them," Gabriel said in a slightly exasperated tone, "since we angels are all telling you the same thing?" A young black woman took the microphone and, her voice shaking with emotion, asked Gabriel whether he really knew how difficult it was for humans to apply his teachings to everyday life. Sympathetically, Gabriel insisted that he understood. "Beloved woman, We have walked beside you in every moment of your pain. We know how difficult it is for you to let go of your illusions and your limitations."

Throughout this dialogue, the congregation's level of emotional involvement had begun to rise noticeably. Gabriel invited anyone in pain to come forward. A score of men and women shuffled into the central aisle, where Sally McIntire stood in front of the podium. As each one came forward, she laced her fingers around the back of the supplicant's neck and bowed her head in silence for half a minute. Then looking the person in the eye, she said quietly, "Go in peace." This continued for ten, then twenty minutes as more people rose from their seats and came forward. The emotional intensity in the room spiralled steadily upward. There was sniffling and soft weeping, and tears streamed down the faces of those standing in the aisle. Others sat with their eyes closed and their hands resting on their knees, palms upward. An eerie, barely audible humming blossomed into an alleluia. Across the room, a soprano vamped on the music, improvising sweetly over the sixteen-bar phrase. When the last person had received Gabriel's healing energy, Sally McIntire returned to her seat in the chancel. For the final minutes of the service, she sat silently, looking dazed. After another song, the woman acting as speaker bid farewell to the congregation. There were hugs and warm goodbyes as people filed past an elderly man shaking hands at the door.

The Temple of Light Ascendant, which is informally affiliated with the National Spiritualist Association of Churches, bears some of the hallmarks of a conventional congregation, including a chatty newsletter flecked with smiley-faces and exclamation points. Although Sally McIntire is obviously the leader of the congregation and the most charismatic channel, several other members of the church regularly act as mediums during Sunday services, diffusing somewhat the Reverend Sally's control over the delivery of spiritual insight. By combining the institutional strength of spiritualist tradition with judicious innovations originating in New Age thought, the Temple of Light

Ascendant has achieved a remarkable degree of stability—one which fosters a level of group catharsis that far outstrips anything I witnessed in other channeling workshops and lectures.

A different approach to the creation of community is taken by the Festival, a nondenominational fellowship in New Mexico that honors all spiritual traditions. Although channeling is not a normal part of the Festival's weekly meetings, several channels mentioned that the congregation had offered them valuable support when they needed the healing powers of a group, and they suggested that it offered an opportunity to see what American churches will look like in the future.

The Festival meets in an auditorium rented from a local civic group. On Sunday mornings it marks the place as its own by hanging a colorful banner outside. In the lobby, members of the congregation leave fliers advertising their services as therapists, bodyworkers, or channels. The welcoming brochure identifies the Festival as "a group of people who are committed to each other's growth, in particular to the realization that each of us is in fact a sacred part of the Oneness of Everything, which is to say part of God." "Beyond this," the document states, "we endorse no particular creed or dogma."

Like the weekly service of the Temple of Light Ascendant, the Festival's liturgy weaves together New Age thought and conventional Christianity. For the first third of the informal ceremony, singing alternates with readings and a healing meditation. After an inspirational message, members of the congregation rise to share whatever is on their minds. The service ends with a candle-lighting ceremony and the singing of an Alleluia while the congregation links hands. The Festival's song list includes chestnuts such as "How Great Thou Art," "Wings of a Dove," and "This Train's Bound for Glory." The meditations, in contrast, were paradigmatic New Age affirmations. During one service, the meditation led participants through images of an ideal lifestyle, thus helping to bring it into being. "I eat food that honors my body and gives me continued good health, because I love myself," prompted the meditation leader. "I engage in work that is well paid, completely fulfilling, and provides me with an opportunity to express myself freely while making the world a better place. I live in a house that is comfortable and expresses love to others and to myself." Another meditation was a journey through the body's cells, molecules, atoms, and subatomic particles, filling all the spaces between them with divine love. Before the collection, the congregation was reminded that giving generously creates a vacuum that can be filled by even greater abundance—an example of something known in New Age circles as "prosperity consciousness." A version of the Lord's Prayer recited regularly at the Festival removes references to hierarchy and patriarchy. Instead of asking God to "forgive us our trespasses," the Festival's version states that we are already forgiven. And rather than being led from temptation, the modified prayer asks that we be led out of separation.

The playful spirit of the congregation can be grasped in an incident that occurred after a scheduled speaker failed to appear. A tanned and fit-looking man named Tom cheerfully agreed to fill in. Facing the congregation, he first proposed a talk on Ayurvedic medicine, to a decidedly tepid response. He then offered to speak on the subject of Tantric sex, a proposal that drew scattered cheers from the sixty people in the auditorium. Over the next fifteen minutes, Tom deftly balanced explicitness and metaphor, dignity and humor, as he delivered a concise lecture on the principles of Tantra: how the flow of male and female energies exchanged in sexual intercourse could heighten pleasure and introduce a truly embodied form of spirituality. Directing his comments to men, Tom insisted that they are obliged to provide women with an unconditional sense of security. This security allows women to experience their sexual birthright, which is multiple orgasms lasting at least five minutes each. A cluster of women in the front rows shouted enthusiastic agreement; several others elbowed their partners. As Tom left the stage to thunderous applause, it was clear that his sermon had spoken directly to the needs and interests of the group.

There are inevitable tensions rippling beneath the Festival's atmosphere of good fellowship. In a region famous for its spiritual entrepreneurs, the time for "personal sharing" in the weekly service is a tempting platform for members who wish to advertise their services. A flier attached to the program asks visitors to refrain from making business announcements. Practical matters occasionally intrude on the flow of healing energy: parking problems, a request for help in cleaning up the auditorium after the service—in short, the small change of communal action.

Whether the Festival's attempt to pour New Age thought into a congregational mold is part of a national trend or simply a unique and successful experiment remains unclear. To some extent, the group rides a powerful current of church growth that began in the eighteenth century and continues today. Although conservative evangelical ministers frequently lament the decline of American religiosity, actual rates of religious adherence in the United States have increased nearly 300 percent since 1776. The past fifty years have seen changes in religious loyalties—the recent shift away from mainstream Protestant denominations to more conservative evangelical churches being one of the most dramatic—and there is evidence that beginning in the 1960s the rate of attendence at religious services of all denominations began a significant decline. Nevertheless, Americans remain a far more churched people than the Founders ever thought possible.[13]

Hidden in attendance figures is a major change in the motivation of churchgoers. Many Americans, especially members of the Baby Boom generation, are now "religious shoppers" who affiliate with congregations not out of a sense of loyalty or family tradition but because they judge a religious group to be most effective in meeting their personal needs. As their needs evolve over the life course, they may change religions several times.[14] This utilitarian focus on the kinds of support that congregations offer to the individual reflects the rise of therapeutic values throughout American society. In *Habits of the Heart,* an influential study of attitudes toward community in the United States, the sociologist Robert Bellah and his co-authors detail the rise of what they call "therapeutic contractualism." Therapeutic contractualism replaces questions of right and wrong with a focus on personal growth. Instead of asking, "Is this morally right?" Americans increasingly ask, "Will this meet my personal needs?" Although the therapeutic perspective is liberating on one level, on another it destabilizes key institutions—family, work, marriage, congregation, neighborhood—which by their nature are incapable of meeting all the needs of everyone who participates in them. Critical relationships thus become subject to constant renegotiation, a process that creates its own inevitable stresses.[15]

The difficulty of reconciling therapeutic contractualism with enduring commitments to others has led to handwringing about the future of community and civic life in the United States. In the much-cited essay "Bowling Alone," Robert D. Putnam, a political scientist, presents evidence showing an alarming decline in civic spirit as measured by such things as voter turnout, union membership, involvement in fraternal and service organizations, and even participation in bowling leagues. Putnam is prominent among those who feel that America's economic and political success over the past two centuries has been due in no small part to a high level of civic engagement among ordinary citizens. Our future prosperity and the integrity of our democratic institutions, he argues, might be threatened if Americans continue their current retreat from civic life.[16]

Other social scientists are less pessimistic than Putnam. Robert Wuthnow, a sociologist who has conducted exhaustive research on the small-group movement, finds that nearly half of the American population has or will have some involvement with a small group that offers "caring and support for its members." He argues that these groups, which he refers to as "modular communities," serve the important purpose of mediating between the individual and large, impersonal institutions. They also counteract what some observers see as the increasing privatization of spirituality, which leads Americans to see faith as a purely private matter lacking a significant collective dimension. While recognizing that support groups can never replace institutions such as the family, Wuthnow maintains that they connect their members to the broader society in constructive ways. Nevertheless, since small groups usually define themselves by the high level of emotional support that they offer to participants, one can reasonably infer that they represent yet another expression of the therapeutic ethos, including its ambivalence about civic life.[17]

At a moment when the nation is pondering its collective commitment to community, both religious and secular, the majority of channels and their clients check in decisively on the side of privatized faith and the valorization of social interactions that qualify as mutually therapeutic. Even a community of worship as flexible as the Festival, essentially a fellowship designed for people who have abandoned churches, imposes too many restrictions for most of those drawn to channeling. Whether channels represent a deviant group on the margins of society or the leading edge of a social trend is still unclear, although I am inclined to believe the latter. More interesting than this antipathy toward institutions is their conviction that governments and churches are artificial social forms, largely perpetuated to gratify the egos of those who run them. Hence the emotional appeal of global community, which would seem to transcend local concerns by focusing on a shared humanity underwritten by the laws of the collective unconscious. Getting there will not be easy, however. Channels frequently commented that the spiritual energies now flooding the earth have had a disorienting effect on society. "People are threatened by the light," Sandy Randolph explained. "That's part of the explanation for the unrest in the cities—the gangs, the violence. Those people aren't ready for the dimensional shift."

Until conditions allow for the expression of a truly global identity, most channels will follow the advice offered by Bryan Wood's spiritual allies, the Clan. "If you wish a society that celebrates the uniqueness of each individual while supporting each individual's right not to be controlled by the choices of others, then your society must be restructured," the Clan insisted. "But the restructuring of your society must begin with the restructuring of your personal life. Focus on changing your own life to celebrate your own uniqueness in a way that makes you happy, and society will follow suit."

7

SPIRITUAL COMMERCE

The tendency of channels and their clients to leap from the individual to the cosmic leaves an immense void in the space usually occupied by the social. People drawn to channeling are likely to view most social institutions as restrictive and artificial. In contrast, they think of direct expert–client relations as transparently natural because they link parties through mutually beneficial exchange. The market, in other words, fills much of the moral space created by the perceived bankruptcy of family, church, and government.

The ubiquity of fee-for-service relationships among practitioners of New Age spirituality has long been a lightning rod for skeptics, who rarely miss an opportunity to deride those who seek money for enlightenment. "Generally speaking," writes Deborah Root, an art historian and cultural critic, "the New Age movement has a blind spot about money, and people involved in these practices tend to see no problem with buying and selling spirituality."[1] Her comments reflect a general uneasiness about the intersection of money and spirituality that springs to the surface when faced by the frank commercialism of some New Age practices. Money changes hands in the most dignified of churches, of course, but institutions discreetly hide the movement of funds from collection plate to pastor. Channels, most of whom are individual entrepreneurs, have no institutional facade behind which to conceal the economic aspect of their relations with clients, hence their vulnerability to the accusation that their motives are primarily financial.

The comments of Deborah Root and other critics of the New Age ignore the intimate ties between religion and business throughout American history. According to the historian William G. McLoughlin, the origin of this alliance can be found in the economic gospel of Puritan settlers, which "dignified and sanctified trade and commerce."[2] Despite the warnings of Puritan clergymen such as Cotton Mather, who held that material gain would tempt faithful Christians to lose sight of God, the nation grew steadily more comfortable with the belief that abundance reflected divine favor and, more important, that piety led to prosperity. The spiritual meaning of wealth was never far from the minds of those who propelled the United States into major religious revivals in the eighteenth and nineteenth centuries. The marketplace itself came to be seen as a vital moral arena, a place where discipline and worthiness were continually put to the test. In a perceptive analysis of the degree to which capitalism has led Americans to attribute moral qualities to market relations, Robert Wuthnow observes that democratic freedoms were increasingly identified with the right of choice, the most common form of which occurs in the daily selection of goods and services. "In exercising that responsibility," Wuthnow argues, "the person can take pride in knowing that he or she has acted as a moral self."[3]

As freelance technicians of the sacred, working channels face the challenges of a volatile market that offers clients a constantly expanding array of therapeutic and spiritual options. To survive and prosper in such an environment, professional channels must learn to broaden their practice, to deal successfully with fickle clients, and to protect their intellectual property within the constraints of New Age values that are hostile to modernity. At the heart of their economic strategies are basic ideas about the spiritual meaning of money.

Among New Age thinkers, money has two faces. The first is that of an artificial human invention responsible for much of the spiritual emptiness and ecological malaise of our times. A vigorous supporter of this view is Marilyn Ferguson, whose best-selling book *The Aquarian Conspiracy* is widely regarded as a manifesto of New Age thought. In a few well-argued paragraphs, Ferguson asserts that money separates us from a grounded understanding of our own creative power while fueling a desire for things that we do not need. Ferguson proposes that whenever possible, we should return to bartering, which nourishes cooperation and focuses attention on the quality of the things we produce; in fact, she says, this process is already under way in co-ops and community-action groups across the nation. At its core, Ferguson's thesis is that money, a human invention, separates us from nature in destructive ways.[4]

Intentionally or not, Ferguson's analysis builds on a long history of Western thought about the moral significance of money, gift-giving, and economic life in general. As the French anthropologist Marcel Mauss pointed out in *The Gift,* a small classic first published in 1925, material goods have always been infused with spiritual and psychological meaning. Among some native peoples, gifts embody the soul of the giver. Others believe that gifts radiate spiritual power. Above all, gifts bind together individuals and groups in a web of exchange. The invention of money undermined this system by replacing the distinctive gift with an abstract measure of value. Writers from Karl Marx to Georg Simmel have commented on money's moral emptiness and its capacity to make all things equal regardless of their intrinsic worth. Tribal peoples are often deeply disturbed by money when they first encounter it, so deeply does it threaten the meaning implicit in gifts. Many view the impersonal, equalizing power of money as unnatural, even obscene.[5]

Among channels and, for that matter, among the majority of people attracted to New Age spirituality, money's sinister face is ignored in favor of a benevolent one. Money is viewed simply as an energy—"accumulated human and planetary creative energy," to be precise—and therefore as a force of nature analogous to gravity, light, or sound waves. By focusing our psychic energies, we can attract the force we call money and think our way to prosperity.[6] Although it would be tempting to attribute such ideas to the modern replacement of physical money by electronic transfers, most arose in the nineteenth century in association with the New Thought movement. Influenced by the founder of Christian Science, Mary Baker Eddy, who preached that God had given human minds the power to triumph over illness and death, New Thought went a step further by proposing that the material world is regulated by spiritual laws. Knowing these laws, the mind can banish false images of scarcity to create abundance. Over time, New Thought percolated into popular philosophies of self-help—notably, the books of Napoleon Hill (author of *Think and Grow Rich,* a best-seller of the 1930s) and Norman Vincent Peale (author of *The Power of*

Positive Thinking). So influential is the idea that attitudes create prosperity that it now plays a central role in American management consulting and in the quasi-religious marketing philosophies of companies such as Amway and Mary Kay Cosmetics.[7]

One of the important legacies of the New Thought movement is a set of techniques called "prosperity consciousness"—essentially, spiritual strategies for attracting wealth. The advertising flier for a prosperity consciousness workshop in Santa Fe, for instance, promised to teach participants how to "magnetize themselves to money" and "reprogram at a cellular level for greater abundance." From this perspective, even financial disaster becomes a spiritual process. A New Age newspaper published in New England recently announced the services of a spiritual counselor who uses shamanistic techniques to provide "non-legal bankruptcy counseling" so that her clients can explore the metaphysical dimensions of their financial distress.[8]

The laws of money and other forms of abundance were outlined in 1993 for an audience of nine people in a half-day workshop led by David and Sasha Johnson. Like many channels, the Johnsons diversify their services by regularly offering classes that call on other areas of expertise. The workshop, entitled "Transforming Lack into Abundance," took place in the basement of their comfortable home in Arizona.

Sasha Johnson began the class by emphasizing that the system she and David were about to describe applies to all forms of abundance, including money, health, free time, and satisfying relationships. When participants introduced themselves, it became clear that their interests bridged all of these concerns, with a slight tilt in the direction of career guidance and a desire for more income. A middle-aged man, for example, described himself as a lawyer who had given up a comfortable legal practice to direct a small foundation. Exhausted by the organization's shaky finances, he was trying to launch a consulting practice. "I'm tired of living on the financial edge," he said. "I'd like a small cushion."

David carefully explained the difference between cravings, which are unhealthy obsessions that lead to suffering, and desires, which he said are perfectly compatible with spiritual growth. He then outlined a seven-step program that can lead an individual from lack to abundance. The steps include an initial self-assessment, making the transition from despair to a plan of action, and keeping prosperity once it is achieved. "You know," David said, "the paradoxical thing about prosperity is that in order to keep it, you have to give it away." Sasha added, "Think of prosperity as energy. You can't stop energy." Elaborating on this theme, they explained that the best way to bring money into your life is to create a space for it. This could mean something as simple as putting extra pocket change in a parking meter—in essence, donating money to the next person who comes along. The same process works for relationships: an occasional kind word to a stranger makes room for friendship in one's own life.

David and Sasha presented these assertions less as moral principles than as neutral laws of the universe. "A river flows because there's stuff coming in and stuff going out," David said. We therefore have to prevent blockages and point the flow in our direction. One good tactic is to identify with nature as much as possible. David said, "In nature there's abundance—more than we can ever imagine. One little mushroom puts out something like five million spores. Everywhere you look there's something trying to grow. So if that's going on in nature, and you're a part of nature, then why not for you too?" He explained that the imagination of human beings creates scarcity amid all this abundance. "Poverty doesn't exist in the universe," he emphasized. "We've created it. It's a nightmare, an illusion, a sleep-state. It's our separation from nature that has produced poverty." Humans who cannot fall into step with the give and take of nature, in other words, are destined to miss nature's bounty. It follows from this that a key to abundance is self-confidence. Here David and Sasha revealed their kinship with earlier proponents of positive thinking. Although it isn't fair, they said, the rich get richer because of their faith that wealth will always find them. Conversely, the poor live with scarcity because of their self-doubt and negativity.

But the lessons imparted by Sasha and David also stressed the cooperative nature of abundance. One of the laws of prosperity is that it must be spread around. David put it this way: "There's no such thing as an island. If your company is prospering when others fall apart, it won't stay prosperous, because you depend on those people to supply you." People need to cooperate with others willing to give and receive aid on the path to abundance. "This thing about being a rugged individualist and clawing your way to the top is bullshit," David insisted. "It's a Western notion that's simply untrue. Everyone relies on others to get what they want."

Self-confidence, generosity, perseverance, a clear vision of the future—these are the qualities that David and Sasha urged their clients to develop in order to attract abundance. "It's not like the economy is out there and you're right here," David said. "The economy is yours. It's a place to play. It all belongs to you."

By denying that abundance and scarcity are caused by specific social and political arrangements, advocates of prosperity consciousness appear to blame poverty on the failings of the poor. But workshops such as the Johnsons' suggest that they are less interested in laying blame for poverty than in finding tactics to escape it. When pushed, most acknowledge that the planet's material resources are by no means inexhaustible. Some even doubt that it would be a good idea for everyone to have all the material things they could possibly want. From the perspective of any individual, however, the amount of wealth available in the world is limitless, just as the grains of sand on a beach are essentially infinite. With the river of prosperity already above flood stage in the land of America's super-rich, it is easy to understand why the less fortunate would hope that some of the backwash can, with a few well-placed sandbags here and there, be diverted in their direction.

The links between money, spirituality, and contemporary American disquiet emerged more clearly during a personal-growth workshop that I attended in Los Angeles in 1993. The event was run by a popular psychologist who has since become a fixture in the world of infomercials, slickly produced television programs that market self-help tapes and videos in the hours before dawn. The ostensible goal of the three-day session was to help the participants make emotional connections to their loved ones. It was a high-performance machine: two hundred paying customers, a dozen facilitators, an administrative team, a sound crew. Participants were led through an increasingly cathartic series of exercises designed to probe their hidden emotions, often by recalling the emotional traumas of childhood, so that they could unmask the "real self" and thereby communicate more effectively with their life-partners. The machinery worked well. At times, the large room was carpeted with tissues left by sobbing men and women. So emotional were some of the exercises that several staff members did nothing but circulate through the room distributing kleenex.

The workshop employed symbols and techniques usually thought of as religious. The workshop's facilitators were identified as "angels" in the registration kit distributed to participants. Much of the gut-wrenching emotional power of the sessions came from extended exercises in guided imagery, accompanied by quiet New Age music, that took participants to imagined places such as their Heart Shrine, a kind of exotic temple in which they praised their inner self for its many virtues. The workshop also made use of repeated declarations of self-love, much like affirmations, intended to inspire greater self-confidence. At the end of the weekend, the angels performed a candlelight ritual that welcomed everyone back to a world that they could now see more clearly, having "opened to love" by ridding themselves of their hidden injuries and false masks. A document distributed to the group succinctly expressed the religious tone of the workshop. Entitled "Decide to Network," it urged participants to redefine themselves as a source of vitality and greatness that can create miracles wherever life takes them.

Despite the workshop's focus on the challenges of relationships, it was soon obvious from personal testimonials that much of the anxiety in the room was occupational. Some participants were marshalling their emotional resources to recover from layoffs in the computer and aerospace industries. Others vented their frustration with corporations that had "downsized" them with no consideration for their commitment and years of service. The fear generated by such an economic sea-change was palpable, especially among the Baby Boomers in the group: at the precise historical moment when they had expected to reap the material fruits of middle age, their economic world is collapsing around them. Yet the workshop offered a vision of how they could adapt to this difficult situation. It promoted precisely the emotional skills needed to move from a corporate setting to the entrepreneurial world: self-confidence, clear personal goals, deftness in making connections to others, and a willingness to sever quickly any ties—to people, to institutions, to communities—that no longer satisfy one's changing needs. It was a perfect introduction to the emotional techniques of therapeutic contractualism.

Because the American economy has shifted sharply in the direction of service industries, middle-class people such as those who attended the California seminar are increasingly expected to tailor their feelings to a set of emotional rules imposed by a job. Positions in sales, public relations, advertising, and management consulting demand emotional work because workers sell themselves and their attitudes as much as they promote a product; in many cases, their attitude *is* the product. Emotional work creates a sense of inner estrangement as people become uncertain about whether their feelings are their own or those demanded by their job.[9]

Both the abundance seminar in Arizona and the personal-growth weekend in California offered techniques for matching work and inner feelings. In slightly different ways, the two workshops advanced the idea that without genuine enthusiasm, it is impossible to remain successful in jobs that demand emotional work. The workshop leaders encouraged participants to find new employment in which they could feel authentic, uncompromised passion for their work—the passion of their "real" selves. In the California seminar, for instance, people were coaxed to stand on their chairs and shout, "I'm taking my power back." Power, in this case, was passion stripped of concern for the feelings of others ("codependency"). Once the real self was back in control, participants were repeatedly told, prosperity and happiness would follow. Because a free-enterprise culture attributes reversals of fortune to the failings of autonomous individuals rather than to social institutions or groups, the present predicament of the middle class is experienced as a profound challenge to the self. Hence the tendency of prosperity seminars to weave together techniques for retooling attitudes and a philosophical stance that restores the sanctity of the self by casting its struggle for wealth, or even just satisfying work, as a spiritual quest.[10]

I interviewed several individuals who claimed to have put spiritual principles to work in their lives and subsequently reaped great economic reward. One, Sarah Denham, identified herself as a former manager at a large computer firm in California's Silicon Valley. Unhappy with her work and anxious to achieve financial independence, she began to apply the teachings of a well-known channel. The channel's message emphasized the human capacity for reshaping the world through conscious processes. By experiencing an intense connection to the universe, it is possible to create the reality that one wants. For Sarah, the techniques worked brilliantly. "I read all the books, and I put a plan into place," she said. "The plan entailed gaining freedom from the computer industry, bringing freedom into my life. I went through conscious creation." This conscious creation brought her a vice presidency in another firm and, shortly thereafter, a million-dollar stock windfall—enough, she felt, to make her financially independent. She now devotes her life to publicizing the books that brought her such abundance. "This material can be world-changing," she insisted. Sarah's story is more dramatic than most, but it reflects a widespread New Age belief that financial success has a spiritual basis and, conversely, that spirituality need make no moral distinction between money and the other energies that animate the universe.

Few working channels have become millionaires before dedicating themselves to the cause of spirit communication, so they must confront the harsh realities of self-employment in a borderline profession. A handful of celebrity channels have been able to parlay their books and workshops into a comfortable living. Perhaps the most successful is Jach Pursel, who speaks for the being named Lazaris. A journalist who attended a Lazaris workshop in Philadelphia estimated that Pursel grossed as much as $180,000 for a weekend workshop in which 300 people enrolled.[11] For every Jach Pursel, however, there are scores, possibly hundreds, of channels who hold meetings that draw only a small crowd for a modest fee—$10 to $20 per person is typical—or an unspecified "love offering." Although private counseling sessions (often referred to as "readings") may bring in $40 to $100 an hour, few of the channels whom I interviewed had enough clients to eke out more than a frugal living, and most also held part-time jobs to support themselves.

Jill Parsons, a channel from Santa Fe, described an average private session. "When the client arrives," she said, "we chat for about fifteen minutes until I get a sense of what the person wants to know. Then I put in a blank tape and channel until the tape recorder clicks off. By then my spirit guides are usually winding down and doing a summation." Jill's guides rarely order clients to do anything specific, although they often provide recommendations. "It's really important," she explained, "that when people leave they feel they've gotten specific tools to work with. They should go away feeling that they have a larger perspective on what's happening in their lives." By listening to tapes made during the reading, clients can clarify points missed during the flow of the session.

Because clients cannot always come in person for counseling, channeled readings are often conducted over the telephone. Jill Parsons explained that telephone work initially made her nervous, but she soon became accustomed to it. A telephone practice, she noted, attracts timid clients who are reluctant to deal with face-to-face counseling. "A while back I channeled for a group of ladies from Louisiana. I never figured out how they heard of me. One of them called, then a couple of days later her friend would call. Just word of mouth—and pretty soon you've done twelve people in Shreveport in one month." A Florida channel who had worked for one of the nationally advertised psychic telephone services claimed that it wasn't difficult to do phone work. "Time and space are illusions anyhow," he said. "From the phone contact I get colors, images, or symbols that allow me to help callers." Nevertheless, he prefers to work with clients in person.

When asked about the ethics of taking money for spiritual guidance, channels typically say that compensation allows them to make their gift available to the world. For them, it is a fact of life that people need money to live, and it follows that they should be paid a reasonable wage for their work. Mary Ann Chase, who has a lively practice in telephone channeling, said, "In the best of all possible worlds, people would give me gifts, like in tribal cultures, where they give gifts of food or whatever. But our world operates by the exchange of money. I've had to make my peace with that." Deborah O'Neill formulated this view differently. She came to recognize her own channeling ability through her friends' repeated requests for readings. "I didn't decide I'd be a channel," she insists. "Everybody *else* decided it. When people come to me, they expect to make an exchange using money, and that's that. So it's not really an issue." When confronted by a client who is financially strapped, Deborah negotiates her fees downward, as do other channels. But she expressed resentment toward clients who shop around for bargain-basement services. For Deborah, the stages of preparing for a reading—scheduling an appointment, saving money to pay the fee, organizing one's thoughts—promote the process of self-discovery that her channeling work is designed to facilitate.

Professional channels explained that money helps to set boundaries for emotionally needy clients. Several reported that they shifted from informal channeling to a more professional therapeutic arrangement after being badgered by clients demanding spiritual guidance during personal crises. A monetary relationship discourages dependency, they insisted. A woman with a full-time counseling practice near San Francisco put it this way: "When you do something for free, people feel that you're universally accessible. People would call at 2 A.M. and ask for channeling because they were having an emergency. There was no sense of boundaries because no one knew what the boundaries were." Money, then, becomes the force that insulates a channel from a client's excessive demands. For their part, clients use the power of money to vote for or against specific channels and the information they convey. Channels whose spiritual sources provide useful information will attract clients and keep them; better information commands higher fees. If a channel's advice proves worthless, clients seek a counselor more in tune with their needs. The unspoken assumption is that market competition fosters spiritual quality control while giving clients maximum freedom to seek the best available guidance.

Issues of intellectual property prove more nettlesome than

does the use of money. Professional channels have a heavy emotional and economic investment in the spirits who provide them with a livelihood. Some entities, especially biblical figures or beings identified in the late nineteenth century by Theosophists such as Madame Blavatsky, have attained the status of public-domain spirits. Across the nation, hundreds of channels speak for them. Spirits of more recent origin tend to be identified with the channel who first brought their message to the world, and it is over these beings that disputes are most likely to arise. Channels often maintain that a given spirit has declared its preference to speak exclusively through them, but such proprietary assertions are notoriously hard to sustain over time, in part because the autonomy of spirits is one of the core beliefs that underlie the worldview of channels and their clients. Some channels have tried to establish their propriety control over spirits by placing a service-mark symbol over the name of their entity and in rare cases by obtaining a legal trademark.

Tension between the independence of spirits and their economic value to the mediums who act as their hosts is revealed in an incident reported by Steven Manning, a successful California channel. Manning speaks for a witty, slightly scandalous spirit named Daniel, whose popularity helped to launch Manning's career. When another channel began to hold public events at which he claimed to speak as Daniel, Manning was forced to ask himself whether he was being exploited. "You know, Daniel is not a copyrighted character," Manning told me. "Whatever I *publish* is copyrighted in my name, but Daniel himself is a spirit. So what am I going to do, copyright a personality?" Manning decided that he first had to determine whether his own copyrighted texts were being acknowledged and quoted correctly by the other channel. He was also curious about the accuracy of the new information coming from his rival. "I eventually met the man who was doing the channeling," Manning said. "I felt that he was getting Daniel at an early phase of his life, when he was more boisterous and more opinionated and a little less mature spiritually than when he speaks through me." In the end, Manning took the high road. "Since I don't have Daniel under exclusive contract, he can appear through other agencies," he said. "You accept it. It broadens the context in which you explore the phenomenon."

Similar situations have arisen elsewhere. Seth, who was first channeled by Jane Roberts in the 1960s and subsequently became the centerpiece of her best-selling books, began to speak through other channels in the 1970s. Frances Morse, a Connecticut woman who claimed to encounter Seth during a near-death experience in 1975, explained that Seth was a "composite energy" that began to provide her with information long before she was ever exposed to the books of Jane Roberts. Clients familiar with the information that Seth gave to Jane Roberts, Frances said, have generally been satisfied with her own version of Seth. Her friends reassure her that "no one owns an energy," and she continues to channel Seth as part of a successful counseling practice.

Two women who work for an organization that disseminates Jane Roberts's teachings, however, expressed guardedly negative opinions about other Seth channels. First, they said, Seth was on record as insisting that he would communicate solely through Jane Roberts. As one put it, "Seth said that only Roberts could maintain the material's integrity." The other offered a more complicated rationale. "Seth talked about how he used Jane's vocabulary, Jane's background, her beingness, to help form who he was," she said. "The entity that channels through a person is going to be uniquely affected by that person's belief system." The being called Seth, then, was a unique alliance of spiritual energies and the personality of Jane Roberts. When Jane Roberts died, this one-of-a-kind collaboration ended, although in theory others might be able to channel sources that are just as insightful. But both women argued strenuously that no other channeled teaching matched the quality of the original Seth material of Jane Roberts. Their mission, as they explained it, was to encourage the diffusion of Seth's philosophy. Yet one can also infer that their organization serves to protect Seth doctrine against contamination by the ideas of outsiders.

The Michael Teachings, a corpus of books that originate in a group of spirits contacted in the 1970s, have taken a different tack by defining themselves as an ongoing, collective venture. Michael is one of the few channeled spirits represented by a foundation: the Michael Educational Foundation (MEF), under whose auspices many Michael channels were trained in the 1980s. According to Marianne Rose, a channel involved with the MEF, the organization once considered setting up formal certification procedures for Michael channels. MEF staff members trained more than a score, many of whom now have full-time channeling practices. This strategy produced something close to franchised channeling. Eventually, however, the Bay Area Michael channels urged the MEF to discontinue the program. They worried that the local market had become saturated, threatening their livelihood.

With so many people channeling the same entity, issues of legitimacy and intellectual property are bound to surface. The MEF must deal with people who claim to be channeling Michael yet produce erroneous information. "These people tend to fall by the wayside," Marianne Rose observed. "If they're truly in touch with Michael, they get very accurate, grounded information. They wind up being popular, and they're able to make a living. If, on the other hand, they're in touch with something or somebody else, it tends to be airy-fairy nonsense." Eventually, clients realize that the information is untrue and seek more accurate guidance elsewhere. According to Rose, inexperienced channels often fall into the trap of sensationalism. "It's easy to get a hint that a rainstorm's coming and think that it's a hurricane," she said. People given to such excesses are, in her words, "self-eliminating." Channels in touch with real Michael information prosper because their insights hold up over time. When the information is right, she said, "you can feel it. It's accurate. It's useful. It works."

Marianne Rose estimated that Michael channels have published nearly a score of books. She alleged that several psychotherapists had "grabbed big chunks" of the Michael Teachings and published them without identifying the source, in part because they feared losing professional standing if their colleagues found out that they were involved in channeling. In general, though, Rose painted a picture of broad collaboration among those in Michael's network.

David and Sasha Johnson, whose practice is based on the Michael Teachings, presented a darker view of the situation. David agreed that what he referred to as "the Michael community" began with an idealistic notion of free exchange and collaborative effort. "But through harsh experience," he said, "we found that information was misused. We had to protect ourselves so that nobody could come around later and say, 'Well, Michael told me to kill someone.'" As a psychotherapist, he was sensitive to his possible liability exposure if the Michael Teachings were implicated in a suicide or some other act of violence.

Sasha, his wife and collaborator, argued that since their writings on the Michael Teachings integrate knowledge from other areas in which she and David have expertise, these published works should be recognized as their intellectual property rather than as Michael's. "What we write is not just pure channeled Michael information," she insisted. "It comes out of our many years of experience." David reported that some of his earlier written work on Michael had been plagiarized. "After a few experiences like that," he admitted, "I felt ripped off. Even though the information is sourced in Michael, the hard work of getting it packaged isn't Michael's. It's our time." David and Sasha allow others to quote or publish their work for free as long as their authorship is acknowledged.

Marianne Rose mentioned that the MEF reminds members that "those who lie or slander or steal someone else's written work will be creating negative karma for themselves that will have to be paid back later." She took pains to emphasize that, as far as the Michael Teachings are concerned, there are no limitations on the number of channels who can contribute to the teachings or on their possible uses. "The more the merrier," she insisted. Yet the creation of a formal organization such as the MEF implicitly asserts control over the flow of information from the collective entity known as Michael, even if it justifies its existence in terms of an ethic of collaboration and exchange.

The comments of Steven Manning, Marianne Rose, and the Johnsons lay bare opposing tendencies in the attitudes of professional channels. Claims of owning a spirit are virtually impossible to sustain. Nevertheless, most channels believe that the work of producing, transcribing, and publishing spirit messages earns them the privilege of asserting copyright. Because spirits cannot be claimed as property, disputes over spiritual ownership must be shifted to a different rhetorical plane—namely, debates about accuracy or authenticity. When Steven Manning heard that another channel was in contact with Daniel, his star spirit, he was skeptical. By concluding that the competitor was channeling a younger version of Daniel, Manning hit on a perfect solution to this potential conflict: he established the superiority of his more "mature" version of Daniel without directly attacking the integrity of his rival.

Lest such debates about spiritual authorship be dismissed as frivolous, it is worth noting that the Library of Congress recognizes spirits as independent authors. The library's catalog has assigned primary authorship to Lazaris and several other spirits, while granting only a supporting role to their channels. As Ted Bernstein, an Arizona channel, learned several years ago, however, the government's recognition of spirits' authorship stops short of willingness to protect their intellectual property. Bernstein reported that his attempt to secure a copyright in the name of his entity was politely rejected on the grounds that current law prevents the assignment of copyright to spirits.

More contentious than the question of spiritual ownership is controversy over the integration of Native American traditions into channeling and other New Age spiritual practices. The conflict pits New Age "wannabe" Indians against Native American traditionalists outraged that their most sacred symbols are being imitated and in some cases commercialized by whites. This cultural borrowing, one Indian writer charges, "is part of a very old story of white racism and genocide against the Indian people."[12]

Although overheated, the rhetoric of Indian activists is grounded in some undisputed facts. In western states, Indian sacred sites on public lands have been virtually taken over, and in some cases damaged, by whites imitating Native American vision quests. Elsewhere, Indian communities have been harmed by the insensitive behavior of tourists seeking religious inspiration. The Huichol of Mexico, for instance, are regularly visited by package tours of Americans who come to participate in the Huichol's annual pilgrimage to collect peyote, a hallucinogenic cactus that plays a key role in native religion. The tours provide income for impoverished Huichols, but they also disrupt community life and subtly change traditional religious behavior. Closer to home, non-Indians claiming membership in such bogus organizations as the Wolf Clan Teaching Lodge regularly offer sweat-lodge ceremonies and drum-making classes. Such infringements anger some Indians, who deeply resent the appropriation of their religion (or a simulated version of it) by outsiders. A few Native American spiritual teachers believe that the world will be a better place if they can help whites to become more like Native Americans. The spiritual elders of intact Indian communities, however, are more likely to conceal their knowledge from outsiders, who in the past have relentlessly suppressed native religions whenever they could.[13]

Although the willingness of whites to perform Indian rituals or to present themselves as teachers of Indian religion may be a new development in the United States, a fascination with Native American spirituality is as old as the republic. Indians regularly visited the nineteenth-century Shakers during the Shakers' trances. In 1842, for example, the Shaker community in Watervliet, New York, played host to 400 unidentified spirit-Indians from Canada, as well as a thousand members of the Chippewa Tribe, including a chief named Shackam and a "chiefess" named Lyda. The most prominent spiritualist of late nineteenth-century Boston, Lenora Piper, counted an Indian maiden with the unlikely name of Chlorine among the spirits she brought forth to impress such distinguished guests as the psychologist William James.[14]

Native American culture appeals to channels, who see Indians as spiritual guides and prophets of ecological salvation. To diversify their professional practice, many seek training in Native American spirituality so that they can add sweat lodges, medicine-wheel rituals, and pipe ceremonies to their list of services. These rites have mostly sprung from the Anglo-American imagination, although they sometimes draw loosely on anthropological accounts or Native American autobiographies. Channels explain their interest in Indian ritual in terms of the ever-changing needs of their spiritual journey, but professional diversification also assures an adequate flow of clients.

One evening in Santa Fe the subject of Native American spirituality arose as people waited for a channeling session to begin. Everyone in the room agreed that it was wrong to become rich by performing Native American rituals and that some of the proceeds of books, lectures, and workshops should be returned to the Indian community. Nevertheless, the group angrily rejected the idea that they must stop performing these rites. Indians, one woman declared, hold key pieces of knowledge that can save the earth from self-destruction. "Indians have maintained an aspect of being, maybe even at a cellular level, that makes them keepers of sacred knowledge that's going to be very important to the planet now," she said. This information is so important that it can no longer be kept a secret. Steve, a middle-aged man who had just moved to New Mexico from California, captured the sentiments of the group when he declared, "Any spiritual essence is put here on the planet to be shared. It's not to be hoarded. Indians have to realize the important role that they're playing." If they agree to share their knowledge with the rest of us, he insisted, their own prosperity will inevitably follow.

The group evidently felt free to exercise a New Age version of eminent domain over Indian religion. The term "birthright" was mentioned when people discussed this process of reclamation. None seemed to recognize how much their rhetoric resembled the promises of a government that has repeatedly urged Indians to give up their lands and natural resources for the good of the nation. Some found it hard to understand why Indians would frame their objections in terms of theft. "How can you steal a religion?" one woman asked, genuinely baffled. "If I try a particular practice from an Indian culture and it touches me deeply, I'm going to keep on doing it."

The edginess of this conversation contrasted with the guileless quality of most New Age ruminations on Indian spirituality. In 1990, for example, I interviewed Sandy Randolph, who has woven Native American themes into her channeling practice in New Mexico. Sandy, who was in her mid-forties at the time of our first interview, has salt-and-pepper hair and a lined face that mark her as someone who has spent the last decade under a western sun. In the 1970s she moved from the midwest to California, where she gravitated to various forms of bodywork and alternative spirituality. When Sandy went on a vision quest in 1983, the spiritual guidance that had long been a presence in her life resolved itself into an image of six elderly American Indian healers, who eventually identified themselves as the Medicine Women. These spirits granted her a personal vision and used their influence to guide her healing work. Their counsel also persuaded her to move to New Mexico, where it "felt like I was aligned with my spirit and my guidance and my direction." To contact the Medicine Women, Sandy has only to enter a light trance. "It's an interesting feeling," she said. "Sometimes it's like the Medicine Women are rifling through my files, my memories, my experiences. They're searching for words or experiences to describe whatever it is they need to say."

In 1990 the intensifying contacts with the Medicine Women had invigorated Sandy's practice as a professional healer, although not enough to free her from part-time work as a sales clerk. An expanding area of her practice is telephone channeling. At first she was unsure how the Medicine Women would respond to telephone consultations. "Initially I was really exhausted by phone readings, as though I were spread out over two thousand miles," she said. "But there has been a shift. It's like the Medicine Women are learning how to spread themselves out so that I'm not exhausted after doing a reading."

Sandy radiated warmth without a hint of dogma. She also had an ability to make the most exotic beliefs sound ordinary, single-handedly reconciling the cultural traditions of Illinois and California. There was an apparent rootlessness about Sandy evident in the succession of jobs, places of residence, and spiritual interests that had marked her life until 1990. When we met again three years later, however, Sandy seemed more settled. She lived in a modest house trailer with a dazzling view of the mountains. Her teaching and healing work were going well enough to provide her with a measure of financial security. She had just returned from a tour of western Europe, where she presented workshops on Native American spirituality. It was possible that the passionate interest in American Indian culture found among the Germans, Swiss, and French could help Sandy find an enthusiastic and affluent clientele, perhaps even a career. The gender of her spiritual guides was an added attraction, as many clients were seeking ratification of their power as women.

In Sandy's innocent and well-meaning fascination with American Indians it is difficult to see the "racism and genocide" that Indian activists find in New Age practices. Her work provides a modest income, but the wisdom of the Medicine Women is not likely to make her wealthy anytime soon. One could argue, I suppose, that any income derived by the teaching of American Indian religion is offensive in an era when so many Indian families live in poverty. But Sandy's parasitizing of Native American culture seems no worse than that of the hundreds of non-Native artists, art dealers, and filmmakers whose livelihood depends on the retailing of Indian likenesses. To some extent, all contribute to the propagation of romanticized images of Native Americans that can have the pernicious effect of de-legitimizing real Indians, who are rarely as colorful and self-evidently "authentic" as their New Age counterparts. Indians run the risk of becoming regarded as inauthentic or corrupted, which can subtly undermine their struggle for land rights and cultural survival in the North American political arena.[15]

These are opening salvos in what is likely to be a protracted debate about the ethics of plagiarizing Native American religions. Thus far the controversy has tended to focus on the alleged "theft" of Indian spirituality—thus treating religion as a form of property—rather than on issues of desecration or disrespect. In a curious case dating to the 1950s, the Zuni Indians of New Mexico formally protested the use of imitation Zuni masks by a group of Boy Scouts in Colorado. Besides insisting that the boys cease their imitation of Zuni dances, the Indians demanded that the masks be turned over to them on the grounds that anything made using Zuni knowledge is the property of the Zuni people, even if the maker is not an Indian. The Zuni recently cited this extraordinary view of ownership in their petition for the return of artifacts collected by the Smithsonian Institution.[16]

The tendency of Indians to use the language of intellectual property to frame protests about the emulation of their spiritual traditions suggests the degree to which they themselves have been affected by the progressive commodification of ideas and images characteristic of late twentieth-century capitalism. When religion is reduced to a technology of personal empowerment—something to be sold in workshops, counseling sessions, books, and videos—it risks becoming a commodity. This process is hardly unique to the New Age; even mainstream denominations now routinely hire marketing experts to help them develop sophisticated campaigns to attract and keep new members.[17] Nevertheless, the New Age case is suffused with an irony at once poignant and bitter: by turning to Native American traditions for models of more vibrant ways to live and to worship, Americans may simultaneously threaten the integrity of Indian spirituality and accelerate the cultural processes that make modern life so disenchanting.

Although most working channels try to cobble together a livelihood through a judicious combination of private readings, telephone sessions, and group workshops, a minority have been successful in combining overtly spiritual work with conventional psychotherapy. This reflects a convergence of alternative spirituality and humanistic psychology that began in the 1960s and has accelerated ever since. (Alternatively, one could read the shift as a renewal of psychology's early links to mesmerism and spiritualism.) Despite concerted efforts by university-educated psychologists and clinical social workers to impose rigorous certification procedures, rapid growth in the number of therapists since the 1965 has made the profession hard to police. Some therapists, especially those struggling for professional survival in a period when cost-conscious heath-maintenance organizations are reducing their counseling staffs, have begun to experiment discreetly with spiritually oriented treatments sought by clients dissatisfied with simple empathy or the healing powers of talk.[18]

In 1994, a group of licensed psychologists and clinical social workers from New England—all middle-aged, middle-class, and holding advanced degrees from major universities—met to talk about the role played by channeling and related "energy work" in their practice. The interview took place in a common room littered with toys used for therapy sessions with children. Deli sandwiches and cartons of Szechuan take-out ranged across a coffee table. The group gathers weekly in this room to share ideas and to help each other meet the challenges of working as outlaws in the borderlands of a regulated profession.[19]

The members of the group met at a series of training seminars offered by a charismatic psychotherapist whose work focused on manipulation of the human aura, an energetic force-field believed by some to emanate from the body. The seminars were a logical extension of their own psychotherapy practices, which regularly dealt with sexual abuse, recovered memory, and spiritual crises of one sort or another. Anita Sanderson, one of the group's leaders, explained that her work with victims of childhood trauma had convinced her that talk therapy is not the most effective way to put clients in touch with their repressed memories. While doing hypnotic inductions, she became sensitive to auras, which she began to visualize with steadily greater clarity. These energy fields, she discovered, could be manipulated to open up her clients to the memories and feelings locked within them. Nancy, another therapist in the group, expanded on this theme. "The most profound thing for me," she said, "is the realization that when a client comes into your office, you're dealing with her energy. All we're doing is trying to gain some mastery of what we're putting out in that energy field. Any therapeutic interchange is energetic."

Anita described how she used this principle in a recent case. "A client with a childhood trauma problem came to me and said, 'I've looked at this issue over and over. If there are other ways to deal with the problem, I'd like to try them today.' All it takes is a direct request like that and—whoosh!—the energy comes through and begins to shift. So we channeled the session. I work with Pleiadian energies as my home frequency. We worked half with my own energies and half with one of her own personal spirit guides." In cases like this one, the guides might reveal long-repressed episodes of childhood sexual abuse or other injuries that damaged the client's energy field. The result, Anita said, was deeply satisfying. "I'm amazed by my clients," she concluded. "They're usually happy with the energy work. It's us, the therapists, who struggle with it all the time." Even after years of practice, she still finds the unorthodox nature of the therapy hard to reconcile with her formal training as a licensed clinical social worker. Her experiences in energy work have gradually moved her from one world—the world of science and ordered medical knowledge—toward something equally powerful but harder to understand.

Several months earlier, I had observed Anita and another member of the group, Katherine, treating a woman caught in the throes of an acute spiritual crisis. Anita, who stood directly in front of the chair in which her patient was seated, began to produce eerie, high-pitched sounds. Katherine took up a position behind the chair and did likewise. Their tones converged, then drifted apart slightly until they had created a powerful interference pattern. The sound felt strong enough to peel paint. The woman who was the target of this sonic blast shook as if she were facing a hurricane. Anita and Katherine moved slowly around her, gently laying their hands on her back, neck, and head. Between bouts of shivering, the woman careened from laughter to sobbing and back again. But the two channels gradually lowered the intensity of their tones and brought the session to a serene conclusion. Contentedly wiping away her tears with a tissue, the woman expressed her gratitude. Katherine later explained that the tones were energy waves from the Pleiades. By directing these sounds at the woman's aura, she said, she and Anita had rebalanced her energy.

Even in the 1990s, insurance companies and HMOs are not ready to endorse the use of energy from the Pleiades, for healing or anything else. They are even less inclined to pay for it. But the members of the energy-work group have managed to dodge the malpractice bullet by billing for these unorthodox therapies only when clients specifically request them. As they cautiously go public with their techniques—say, by adding the term "energy work" to business cards—clients seek them out precisely because they want to explore new therapeutic territory. With an accent that betrayed her Boston Irish origins, Maureen, another member of the group, asserted that she is now so committed to channeling and energy work that she wouldn't care if her license were revoked. "It feels to me that a higher power intends for me to do this work," she said. "I'll be provided with opportunities to support myself, whether it's with a license or not."

The group is more concerned with issues of professional standing than with licensing. They are clearly proud of their rig-

orous training and reluctant to cut their ties to colleagues committed to conventional therapy. Don, one of two men at the
meeting, argued that graduate training serves an important
gate-keeping function by preventing quacks from entering the
profession. Katherine and some of the others joked about what
they called the "fruitcake scale," an index of looniness that they
applied to certain therapies promoted at alternative-health fairs.
With good reason, they worried that their peers would assign
them a high score on this scale. "We're sitting here talking
about things that most of our colleagues would say were reason
for commitment to a mental hospital," one of them tossed off
with a laugh. James, a psychologist trained in Europe, admitted
that it had been harder for him to come out publicly as a channel than as a gay man. Their weekly meetings help to bolster
everyone's spirits when the burden of being discreet about their
healing work overwhelms them. They also use the meetings to
practice healing each other. On the rare occasions when they
give presentations to other professionals in the mental-health
field, they tend to deal with energy work tangentially under the
rubric of "bringing spirituality into psychotherapy."

When asked how they determine the validity of what they're
doing once they've jettisoned the standards of science, they
reply that the only standard worth upholding is whether clients
heal. Katherine spoke up: "That's the amazing thing. People get
better a lot faster. I can teach them to read their own energy
field: there's a block here, a problem there. This *works!* They
feel better. They have more joy in their lives." Here Maureen
jumped in. "And when you identify what's going on with them,
they know what you're talking about," she said. "They express
such relief: 'Oh, somebody finally understands.'" Diane was
even more emphatic: "People are phenomenally open to this

work. It hits a place in their hearts that feels right to them. They open their heart and embrace it."

Although the members of the group criticized the limiting nature of conventional treatment strategies, they were careful to emphasize that channeling and other forms of energy work are additions to traditional psychotherapy, not replacements for it. "I've always felt enriched by my formal training," Anita said, "and I'm much more confident about moving into other kinds of work because I'm grounded in that tradition." All of them continue to engage in conventional talk therapy, but as word of their use of channeling spreads, the number of clients who come to them for spiritual treatment steadily increases. Katherine said that although only about ten percent of her clients are ready to be treated with channeled tones, about eighty percent are willing to work with their energy fields. Anita estimated that half of her practice involved energy work. Because Katherine also holds a divinity degree, she gets referrals for clients wrestling with spiritual issues. They appear in her office and declare, "I'd like you to help me find my spiritual path," or "I want to know how to experience God's presence in my life," or "I'd like to get in touch with my spirit guides."

This group of nonconforming psychotherapists enjoys a comfortable flow of clients, and others are beginning to seek them out. They are articulate and enthusiastic proponents of the view that the most effective way to heal the injuries of this lifetime is to open ourselves to forces originating in other times, dimensions, and galaxies. The issues at the heart of their work—dissociation, recovered memory, the treatment of fragmented selves—are part of a growth industry in spiritualized forms of health care and emotional therapy that attract the middle class in growing numbers. As Baby Boomers, the largest and most affluent demographic cohort in American history, begin to wrestle with their own mortality, channeling therapists and others like them will be well positioned to meet demand for self-exploration delivered in an organized, businesslike manner.

The history of alternative religious movements in nineteenth- and twentieth-century America suggests that many survive by avoiding a direct confrontation with mainstream religions, occupying instead a different social niche: that of therapy.[20] Channeling and related practices have clearly moved in this direction, as a glance at any regional New Age magazine will confirm. But the economic and social environment of the 1990s is distinct from that of the 1890s or even the 1950s. Ours is a moment in which virtually anything can become a valuable asset in a chain of market relations: life forms, brand names, memorable images, modes of healing, even the spiritual legacy of other cultures. When channels seek trademark protection for the spirits that provide them with a livelihood, or expect payment in return for services, they simply act like other professionals. The difference is that unlike their counterparts in law, finance, and medicine, channels cannot hide the commercial nature of their transactions behind the decorated pediments of a corporate headquarters or the burnished words of a publicist. Their clients, who reflect the new religious consumerism of our time, pursue advice and treatment to address constantly shifting needs. Today their therapy might include channeling, tomorrow Ayurvedic medicine or Qigong. If channeling sometimes looks more like a boutique in the shopping mall of the New Age than it does a religious movement grounded in shared commitment and a sharply defined moral vision, it is because it mirrors so perfectly the society in which it has arisen.

8

BEING MULTIPLE

Nancy Graham lives several miles from the center of a picturesque village in western Connecticut. Her driveway, scarcely more than a logging trail that veers off a corrugated county road, descends a hundred yards to a fairy-tale cottage surrounded by rambling gardens and forest. Nancy is a fit-looking 45-year-old woman who tends her small patch of Eden in the company of two cats and a dog.

Nancy served strong coffee in her living room as she shared her life history, a story of middle-class travail and ongoing redemption: a Roman Catholic upbringing, from which she is now distanced; marriage; a painful divorce fifteen years ago; the loss of her mother to cancer a few years later; the decision to reclaim a life of self-sufficiency and intimacy with nature by moving to the country. She lives simply, supporting herself by part-time jobs and, more recently, by taking a full-time position in state government. Since moving to the cottage, she has focused on her own spiritual development, both by working with others in small groups or by spending time alone in quiet contemplation. "I'm committed to the idea that a spiritual path is something that one walks alone. I want to access that part of myself," she said. Her devotion to personal growth has prevented her from remarrying, but she is now warming to the idea of forming a stable partnership with a man.

During periods of meditation ten years ago, Nancy began to hear the voice of another being and to let it speak through her. She first became aware of the voice, she said, while meditating on the word "open" and calling to her dead mother in her thoughts. After this initial experience of connection, the voice spoke to her regularly in what she described as poetic language. She experienced it as "the universal oneness." Later she channeled other forms of consciousness: the spirits of rocks, trees, and animals, and occasionally the souls of the dead. Her description of these experiences jumped haphazardly from one theme to another; unlike many professional channels, Nancy had not yet worn off the rough edges of her story through repeated telling.

Nancy insisted that her new-found channeling gift helped to renew her links to nature, making her feel part of the earth's cycles. At first she thought that channeling put her in touch with external energies of some kind, but now she has come to think of it as an opening to her higher self. "I see myself as God," she told me. "When I go to that altered state, I tap into a space where everything *is*—where it just is, where everything exists, where the energy begins." Lately, however, she has moved away from channeling toward the application of its insights to her daily life, a shift that parallels the decision to return to the high-pressure world of government service. "The message only lives if you embody it," she emphasized.

Although Nancy claimed to have had little direct involvement with New Age spirituality, she voiced themes addressed by people who make their living by talking to and for spirits. Her life history bore the stamp of deep conviction and echoed the stories of other channels. One can read this narrative as a tale of dislocation: divorce, a mother's untimely death, intentional exile. Nancy launched herself on a search for inner resources and a way to reconnect to the natural world. The result was a sense of self-expansion and a growing awareness of her own divinity. Nancy's declaration that she is God will sound like megalomania to some, but for her, and for the many people involved in channeling who make similar statements, it expresses a sense of infinite personal possibilities, not a desire to rule the world. For Nancy, the self has expanded to fill the space left by the evaporation of vital social bonds. Now she feels ready to apply her amplified self to the challenges of life in an urban workplace.

Her narrative of self-expansion draws on powerful currents in American culture. Nancy's view of persons as eternal, continually remaking and improving themselves in a world of unlimited possibilities, was observed by Alexis de Tocqueville during his travels through the young United States in the early nineteenth century. What de Tocqueville called the "philosophical approach of the Americans" included a strong desire to break free of established molds, to repudiate tradition, and "to seek by themselves and in themselves for the only reason for things."[1] In the twentieth century, this search has led the self to splinter like the shards of a broken mirror. The psychiatrist Robert Jay Lifton refers to the fragmented self as protean, after the Greek sea god Proteus, who could magically assume different forms. Lifton sees the unstable quality of the self—its "radical fluidity"—as the essential psychological trait of our time, a response to a world changing at an unprecedented rate. To survive, both physically and emotionally, we must take on multiple guises, change jobs and residences and nationalities, and struggle to find moral meaning as the ground shifts beneath our feet. One of the paradoxes of the protean self is that it simultaneously seeks multidimensionality and unity. It is, as Lifton puts it, "a balancing act between responsive shapeshifting, on the one hand, and efforts to consolidate and cohere, on the other."[2] The underlying cultural currents that produced the protean self have given rise to diverse philosophical, therapeutic, and spiritual settings in which a preoccupation with self-fragmentation takes center stage.

One such arena is the world of computer-mediated communication. For many of those who flock to the Internet, the attraction of the online domain is less the possibility of boundless connection than it is the chance to take on new identities, thus reconnoitering exotic regions of the self. Sherry Turkle, a canny observer of on-line psychology, notes that the window-based interface that today plays a key role in most popular computer programs has become a central metaphor for the simultaneous representation of different identities by the same person. "The life practice of windows is that of a decentered self that exists in many worlds and plays many roles at the same time," she writes. For Turkle, online windowing is symptomatic of our collective movement in the direction of the postmodern psychology articulated by Jacques Lacan, Gilles Deleuze, and other mandarins of late twentieth-century French philosophy. The postmodern self is fragmented, kaleidoscopic, a frail web of linguistic allusions; it is, in other words, whatever it pretends to be. Such a self finds a perfect home in Internet multi-user domains, where participants engage in a process of world-creation untroubled by the artificiality of their cooperative venture. "In the culture of simulation," Turkle observes, "if it works for you, it has all the reality it needs."[3]

Earlier I discussed the convergence of notions of global community offered by Internet prophets and those articulated by channels and their clients. They also share similar ideas about the emergent and multiplex nature of the self. Channels speak frequently of the multidimensional aspects of identity, for instance, or the possibility that we are simultaneously co-existing on different planes. The person who succeeds in linking up to a "higher self" experiences this as more real than the limited, bounded self of everyday life. The overlap in self-concepts between two such apparently different groups—religious seekers expressing intense nostalgia for our tribal past and computer users scouting the cutting edge of capitalist technology—suggests the pervasiveness of the cultural currents fostering a preoccupation with self-fragmentation and multiplicity.[4]

The particular spin that channels put on the multiple self differs in some respects from the on-line version described by Turkle. Although channels are often playful in their approach to self-multiplicity, most are committed to the goal of connecting to a deeper reality. Indeed, their quest is as much as anything a search for authenticity, by which they mean a primordial sense of wholeness and connection. (Ironically, to find wholeness they first seek fragmentation, which leads to revelations about the multiple facets of an expanded self.) Commitment to the idea of an ultimate reality is evident in the efforts by channels such as Kevin Ryerson to provide "objective" proof that their spirit entities once existed on earth. Others search the daily news for confirmation that the prophecies of their spirit guides are actually coming to pass. Nevertheless, many people involved in channeling are as pragmatic as their online counterparts. If a belief helps to make their lives happier, the question of whether it can be verified by secular truth standards is of little concern.

One could protest that because channeling has affinities to American spiritualism and, more distantly, to techniques of spirit possession and mediumship found elsewhere, its present renaissance cannot be attributed solely to contemporary social conditions. This objection has merit, as does the complaint that philosophers have overstated the distinction between an allegedly coherent modern self and a splintered postmodern one. Nevertheless, channeling's obsession with personal identity marks it as a significant departure from other versions of mediumship and possession. Nineteenth-century spiritualism, for example, was oriented to public edification, not personal growth. Spiritualists envisioned the afterlife as a celestial continuation of pastoral America, a quaint New England village in which the spirits of deceased children were taught to read and write by gentle nannies.[5] In contrast, channels elaborate a vision of the spirit realm that bears little resemblance to America or even to Earth. Gone are the central features of human life, including gender, class, and the key moral distinctions of the social world. If the spheres, dimensions, or planets occupied by spirit entities are described at all, they appear as featureless spaces presided over by an omnicompetent celestial bureaucracy. Spiritualists were deeply committed to the distinctiveness of their spirit contacts, whereas many channels think of their entities as extensions of an expanding self. This sentiment was clearly underscored in a recent flier for a lecture that promised participants "a direct experience of the self as the whole Universe."

Although artists, channels, and members of the online community apparently experience self-multiplication as profoundly liberating, for others it can be disorienting. Bewilderment over the boundaries of self veers into pathology in the condition known as multiple personality disorder. People diagnosed as multiples typically exhibit sharp changes in expressive behavior that segregate into distinct, consistent personalities or "alters." Oscillation among different alters is often accompanied by amnesia in which the victim's original self (variously referred to as the "birth person," "main alter," or "core personality") cannot recall events that occur when a secondary alter takes control. Such dramatic identity shifts eventually provoke anxiety and emotional paralysis.

Before 1980 only about 200 cases of multiple personality had been documented in the world psychiatric literature. Reported cases began to proliferate in the 1980s, and by 1991 a clinician could propose in a respectable journal that one percent of North American adults may suffer from it, implying that undiagnosed cases number in the millions.[6] As the number of multiple-personality cases has increased, so has the number of alters expressed by the afflicted. Early cases in the literature reported two or three distinct personalities, but today victims routinely exhibit dozens; alter constellations, consisting of hundreds of separate personality fragments, are by no means unknown. Although psychologists continue to debate the exact etiology of multiple personality, most believe that the condition arises from childhood abuse, often of a sexual nature. Like other serious illnesses, multiple personality has spawned a large self-help literature, including newsletters dedicated to the exploration "of the many selves inside us."

To an anthropologist, multiple personality looks suspiciously like a culture-bound syndrome, a condition created through subtle interactions between individuals and the institutions that shape their experience. Widely diagnosed in the United States and Canada, multiple personality is virtually unknown in most of Europe and Asia. Even in the countries where it is most often found, it has mutated from a rare and exotic condition to a common one in less than two decades. Its demographic profile is markedly skewed: nearly 90 percent of multiples are women. Such an unusual epidemiology has led to heated debate among experts about whether multiple personality exists as a real malady or instead represents an iatrogenic condition—that is, an illness created by therapists, who unconsciously encourage expressions of multiplicity in emotionally fragile clients. The philosopher Ian Hacking proposes that the concept of multiple personality creates "a new way to be an unhappy person" by offering a language in which the expression of unhappiness can take a concrete form. To this sensible observation one might add that the specific manifestation of anxiety at issue here is the fragmentation of self, the conviction that other aspects of one's personality are emerging in sufficient clarity that they should be given distinct names.[7]

Channeling and multiple personality clearly have different emotional trajectories and implications for those who experience them, yet the idioms in which they are discussed reveal striking parallels. Clinicians urge therapists to treat each alter personality as if it were a separate being with distinct emotional problems, an approach that some trance channels take with their spirit entities. The literature on multiple personality makes frequent reference to a key alter called the Inner Self-Helper, a wise personality who acts in the best interests of the whole person, much as guardian angels or spirit guides protect their human wards. Bennett G. Braun, a psychiatrist prominent in the field of multiple personality, argues that the therapist's goal in treating the condition should not be the elimination of alters but instead the achievement of "co-consciousness and integration," terms frequently invoked by channels when describing their relationship to spirits. Braun's language can be read as implying that self-fragmentation need not be cured, only domesticated. This theme is picked up in self-help literature penned by multiples, many of whom reject the view that their condition is a disorder—the term is too "disempowering," they insist—and instead celebrate the special qualities with which their multiplicity imbues them.[8]

The over-representation of women among channels is mirrored in the phenomenon of multiple personality. As channels, women are free to assert religious authority and to experience a liberating androgyny, but few advantages accrue to multiple personality. Because childhood trauma is held to a key precipitating factor, most therapists account for the lopsided gender ratio among multiples by attributing it to the far greater likelihood that girls will be victims of sexual abuse. One can reasonably infer that the growing frequency with which multiple personality is diagnosed in North America is driven at least in part by the perception, amounting to a moral panic, that sexual abuse of children is now rampant in American society.

Janice Haaken, a feminist psychologist, suggests an alternative framework. While allowing that sexual trauma may be a factor in many cases of multiple personality, Haaken argues that women may be especially prone to dissociative disorders because of the social conditions that prevail throughout their life course. "Dissociation not only is a defense against trauma but also can be a defense against a world that holds one captive without providing sufficient integrative possibilities or pleasure," she asserts. Because of what Haaken characterizes as "fragmenting discontinuities" in their lives, women are more likely to express dissociation in the chaotic form associated with multiple personality. Haaken implies that the trauma-based model of multiple personality is attractive to therapists and clients because it focuses on a specific evil instead of diffuse cultural forces that are far more difficult to pinpoint and change.[9]

Psychiatry has thus medicalized the protean self, giving it a special language, a symptomatology, a regime of therapy. Channels, in contrast, celebrate it. Baffled by the multitudes within themselves, channels and their clients reach into the depths of the unconscious for stories that explain their multiplicity. Explanations emerge as tales of past lives, parallel identities on other dimensions, or thrilling encounters with aliens. Not only does channeling provide satisfying explanations for our changeable selves, it allows channels to embody these selves, giving voice to their thoughts, flesh and bone to their gestures. Admittedly, the audience at a channeling session experiences this only vicariously, but at the very least they witness a dramatic portrayal of the protean currents in their own experience.

Multiplicity as affliction and as emergent possibility: the two converge in the work of Anita Sanderson and the other channeling therapists with whom she practices "energy work." It was probably inevitable that as alter personalities multiplied in patients, they would also begin to proliferate in their therapists as well. In any event, Anita and her colleagues enthusiastically embrace their own multiplex nature, seeing it as a resource for healing. This signals to their clients that multiple inner voices are an acceptable, even a desirable, part of self-understanding and personal growth. These voices are not the alters of multiple personality, fragments of the self allegedly born in pain and helplessness, but instead hidden facets of a grander self whose reflections reach out to other places, times, and dimensions.

Like those who conquer a fear of heights by taking up skydiving, channels actively seek fragmentation of the self so that they can redefine the process as something under their control. Control is hardly an alien theme to middle-class Americans. We struggle to reshape our bodies through exercise and to cultivate the habits of highly effective people. We draft speech codes to protect ourselves from offensive ideas; gated housing developments shelter us from offensive persons. We talk constantly about "empowerment," a codeword for greater mastery of the social world. If bad things happen to us, there must be someone to blame, even if it is only ourselves. Channeling ratchets these sentiments up a notch by proposing that the indignities still lying beyond conscious control—notably, death, as well as life-threatening diseases and injuries—are hardships chosen by our "real" self as part of a process of spiritual education. Whatever happens, we (that is, our "real" selves) are still in charge, although we may not realize it. In that sense, we are divine beings.

Tied to the idea that each of us authors our own text is the belief that we do it alone. In the worldview of channels and their clients, society serves no purpose other than to cripple us with a false sense of limitation. Ultimately, we are responsible only for ourselves, and we must create our own future individually.[10] Like many Americans drawn to alternative spirituality, channels want to leap from the personal to the universal, bypassing society itself. It is only a slight exaggeration to say that many dream of community without society.

Again, although channeling offers a radical version of this asocial view of human destiny, the sentiments that underlie it are shared by the millions of Americans who reject social explanations for unemployment, poverty, and crime, and who see individual advancement as the nation's sole moral imperative. Deep ambivalence toward society, in fact, goes far beyond the

New Age movement. The essayist Lewis Lapham has observed that for a democracy such as ours to survive, it needs face-to-face encounters in which citizens iron out their differences through dialogue and compromise. Yet increasingly segmented communication technologies—cable television, for instance, or the thousands of specialized discussion groups on the Internet—now allow us to "retreat into the sanctuaries of the self," limiting contacts with voices different from our own. This fosters the spread of self-referential groups that seem to inhabit a parallel universe: right-wing militias, apocalyptic cults, and single-issue enthusiasts of every description.[11] Channeling draws on this fragmenting *zeitgeist,* although it is by no means its most alarming manifestation.

As the point of intersection between society and spirituality, institutionalized religion is singled out for the fiercest criticism by those involved in channeling. But they are hardly the first Americans to want their religion first-hand, untainted by clergy or creed. Scholars of American religion suggest that the steady growth of new forms of spirituality may have less to do with collective angst than with the stifling effect of bureaucratic control. As a form of activity protected by the Constitution, religion is one of the last remaining frontiers of personal experimentation, a place where people can explore ideas and social arrangements that would be prohibited in other spheres of life.[12] When the participants in Deborah O'Neill's channeling workshop established their own contacts with Spirit, they followed a tradition of American religious democracy at least two centuries old.

The postmodern elements in channeling performances should not blind us to their powerful modernist premise. Channels and their clients believe passionately in the idea of progress, both personal and cosmic. We and the universe are going somewhere,

somewhere better. Individual lives are tales of what the Archangel Gabriel, speaking at the Temple of Light Ascendant, called "evolvement," an inexorable, if sometimes arduous, journey to perfection. Instead of seeing multidimensionality as a quality that shatters the self, channels cling to it as proof of their all-encompassing wholeness. Although only a minority of those involved in channeling are attracted to prophecies of doom, most accept that we are undergoing a global transformation that will soon end life as we know it. A message posted in an on-line discussion forum devoted to channeling put this in emphatic terms. "Something *is* happening and *will* happen soon," the author insisted. "So you people out there receiving information to help others, let's hear it please." Channeling, in other words, is seen as a source of prophecy and insight that will help humankind face this difficult future.[13]

On balance, channels and their clients tend to be optimists for whom all things seem possible and all horizons limitless. They are voracious readers of everything from theology to science fiction, with intermediate stops in the worlds of self-help, non-Western religions, mythology, evolutionary biology, the occult, and particle physics. Many display the unruly enthusiasms of the self-educated—meaning, among other things, that they are capable of jumping with dizzying speed from, say, Maya prophecy to immunology, sometimes in the same sentence. Their restless curiosity calls into question the belief that middle-class Americans are interested only in the amusements that arrive through their television cables. Over time, I came to admire their exuberance and creativity, precious commodities in a society that suddenly seems unsure of itself.

But channeling has a troubling side as well. Its relentless focus on human universals provides little guidance about how to deal with the cultural differences that tear at the fabric of our society. Along with others involved in New Age spirituality, many channels are reluctant to make the critical judgments that help to discern whether one idea is better than another or even to propose a framework within which such necessary discriminations can be made. An obsession with self raises questions about the prospects of a nation that desperately needs a sense of collective purpose; for all the talk about community, I witnessed few practical efforts to apply channeling's insights to the solution of social problems. The anarchic quality of channeling's theology, with its ever proliferating ranks of spirits, can make one feel like the victim of a British soccer riot, crushed against a chain-link fence by stampeding entities: Ramtha, Mafu, Emmanuel, Lazaris, the Pleiadians, the Wise Ones, Michael, Tom MacPherson, Atun-Re, the Clan, the Archangel Gabriel, Master Maitreya, Seth, Kumar, Ashtar, Saint Germain, Mary Magdalena, Dwahl Khul, sundry Ascended Masters and fifth-dimensional beings and Native American healers—in short, a United Nations of invisible presences that, despite their burgeoning numbers, fail to offer a precise map for the creation of moral communities, without which meaningful spirituality is impossible.

Opinions vary about channeling's future in the changing kaleidoscope of contemporary American religion. A prominent scholar of religious studies has identified channeling as the New Age practice with the best prospects of long-term survival. In his view, channels with large followings will seek greater stability by forming groups that resemble traditional churches.[14] This strikes me as doubtful. Although the disciples of charismatic channels sometimes coalesce into reasonably stable groups, history has shown that channeling is by its nature too democratic to be controlled by anyone for long. Any members of the congregation willing to open their minds to the messages that wait within can forge their own personal links to divine beings, thus undermining the prevailing orthodoxy.

A more likely prospect is that channeling will diffuse into the cultural mainstream, absorbed by the personal-growth movement and the rapid spread of alternative healing methods. To some extent, this has already happened: as channels shift from trance to conscious channeling, it becomes more difficult to distinguish what they do from various forms of meditation or guided-imagery therapy. In a more diluted form, channeling also seems destined to diffuse into the outer reaches of contemporary psychotherapy, especially among therapists willing to address their clients' spiritual needs. Channels themselves are convinced that their gift will eventually be an ordinary part of human life. Some see this as the recovery of an ancient birthright, others as the next step in human evolution. Either way, they claim to be happy to contemplate their own obsolescence. "Sooner or later there won't be any channels to consult," one practitioner insisted, "because everybody will be channeling all the time."

My last venture into the field before bringing the channeling research to a close was an event organized by Anita Sanderson and her colleagues in 1995. She and her fellow therapists are part of a larger group that experiments with channeling, taking it far beyond its potential uses as a counseling tool. The group decided to share their discoveries with an audience of family and sympathetic friends. Sixty people gathered in a church activity room to find out what Anita and her friends had been up to for the past several years.

For nearly three hours we witnessed channeling in several forms. Anita gave voice to the Pleiadians, the extraterrestrials whom she identifies as the main source of her inspiration. Another woman spoke as a Native American healer. The dozen-or-so members of the channeling collective emitted polyphonic tones for fifteen minutes at a stretch. The sounds ricocheted off the ceiling, sometimes dopplering like a train whistle in the night, sometimes settling into a murmur punctuated by treble squeals and sibilant whooshing sounds.

Toward the end of the event, Anita slipped into a different voice, the extravagant Southern accent of a spirit called Belle. Unlike the decorous Pleiadians, Belle spoke in an earthy vernacular. Her role, she said, is to prod humans out of their doubt or complacency. This is necessary because the earth and its inhabitants are facing a moment of great change when impossible things will become possible, perhaps even necessary. She then broached a theme that tied together channeling and Internet identity-bending and multiple personality and other manifestations of self-fragmentation to which modernity has given rise. "I'm hoping that you're willing to let yourself listen to some of the things that go on inside your head," she said, referring to the inner voices that for many seem to be speaking with steadily growing intensity. "We're all hoping that you can be more open to what you *know* is really going on around you. Are you willing to listen to that voice telling you something important?" With that question she assured us that we must welcome the inner selves that can, if we only take them seriously, lead us to greater understanding and even to happiness. "You might think you'd be foolish to go around listening to things inside your head or watching for signs or making something of things that other people don't think have much importance," Belle said confidently. "But if you begin to do that, you'll realize how foolish you were when you weren't listening and watching."

Her words, which manage to evince both irony and a millenarian enthusiasm, illustrate channeling's promise as well as its limitations. At its best, channeling offers fertile ground for play—not in the sense of foolish amusement, although some will insist on seeing it that way, but something closer to Johan Huizinga's definition of play as "voluntary activity . . . having its aim in itself and accompanied by a feeling of tension, joy and the consciousness that it is 'different' from 'ordinary life.'"[15] A notable feature of many channeling events is the prevalence of subtle meta-messages that say, in effect, "I am playing at being a spirit." One sees this in the ubiquitous word-play of channeling performances, including the frequent jokes about the dilemmas faced by spirit entities when they find themselves in unfamiliar human bodies. Play, Huizinga notes, is about freedom and indeterminacy. Channels and their clients play with eternal what-ifs: What if I am part of a larger spiritual plan? How would it feel to be of a different gender? What might I learn by listening to the parts of my inner conversation silenced by the demands of daily life? What will happen if I pretend, perhaps only for a moment, that I can perform miracles? Just as the inner logic of games can be immensely satisfying to players, so the play central to channeling, dependent as it is on the voluntary suspension of everyday rules, can yield pleasures, insights, occasionally even its own purifying catharsis.

Yet like all games, channeling's improvisational vigor depends on a constraining structure, a social order against which it can exercise its inventive energy. Denied an oppositional framework, it quickly takes on the rigid authority of received truth or spins off into self-important apocalyptic babble. In a society that turns ideas into commodities, channeling's creativity easily gives way to shameless commercialism, a shift that critics claim to see in the practices of highly paid celebrity channels. Provided that such perils can be avoided, channeling and related techniques of self-expansion will continue to offer a lively arena for the free play of the religious imagination. Committed rationalists will never find the channeling zone an attractive destination, except perhaps as a place to replenish their store of cautionary tales. For countless others, however, it is likely to remain a site of emotional and spiritual renewal in a culture that, perhaps more than any in human history, promotes the continuous reinvention of the self.

NOTES

Sources on Contemporary American Channeling

The history of human communication with spirits has been chronicled in many places. Notable among recent works are Klimo, *Channeling*; Hastings, *With the Tongues of Men and Angels*; and Riordan's admirably concise entry under "Channeling" in Melton et al., *New Age Encyclopedia*. Although these experts see channeling as a modern version of spirit possession, shamanism, and forms of divination practiced since ancient times, the increasingly generic quality of its theology and the commercial manner of its distribution reveal the degree to which channeling has been reshaped by urbanization and mass literacy. The number of people exposed to the messages of channels in books and videos exceeds by an order of magnitude those who have witnessed channeling in person.

Probably the most prolific channel in American history is Edgar Cayce (1877–1945). Cayce, a photographer, dabbled in occult teachings and alternative healing methods until the early 1920s, when he began to give psychic readings that produced detailed information about reincarnation, health, psychic powers, and the future of humanity. Thousands of pages of his readings are today archived by the Association for Research and Enlightenment, Inc., in Virginia Beach, Virginia. Cayce's published works, many of which are still in print, offer thoughts on everything from homeopathy and reincarnation to Atlantis and Egypt. His contribution to contemporary channeling lies as much in his eclectic sensibility as in any specific message.

Channeling in its present form appeared on the American scene beginning in the early 1970s, identified closely with the work of Jane Roberts, Ken Carey, J. Z. Knight, Kevin Ryerson, Pat Rodegast, and, more recently, Jack Pursel and Barbara Marciniak, each of whom has published books claiming to transmit the wisdom of the author's spiritual allies. The last three decades have seen an explosive growth in the amount of channeled material available in print, thus reversing the occult turn in spiritualism led by Theosophy. (Bjorling's comprehensive bibliography, *Channeling,* contains more than 2,700 entries, most of which have appeared since 1965.)

As channeling emerged in its present form, channeled texts shed the Old Testament language of spiritualist tracts in favor of speech that is plainer and more concise, if still ponderous. The 1200-page *A Course in Miracles* (1975), for example, maintains a biblical heft consistent with the identity of its celestial author, whom the text implies is Jesus of Nazareth, yet it is written in an unadorned, first-person prose style and includes a teaching manual and workbook that bring spiritual issues down to a practical level.

More typical of contemporary texts are the books of Jane Roberts (1929–1984), including *The Seth Material* (1970) and *Seth Speaks* (1972), which convey a sense of the lively, interactive quality of most channeling sessions. The Seth books, like other popular channeled works published since, have spawned an extensive secondary literature, as well as audio tapes, videos, online discussion groups, magazines, and regional conferences. Virtually every channel within reach of a photocopy machine and a tape recorder can become a publisher, and it would seem that most do.

One reason for channeling's rapid diffusion into the American mainstream is the ready availability of how-to courses—often with titles like "Connecting to Personal Guides" or "Getting in Touch with Guidance"—at personal-growth centers across the nation. Books that provide practical hints on channeling include Andrews, *How to Meet and Work with Spirit Guides,* and Ridall, *Channeling.*

New channeled material continues to appear in several widely distributed magazines, among them the *SEDONA Journal of EMERGENCE!* (P.O. Box 1526, Sedona, AZ 86339), *Connecting Link* (9392 Whitneyville Rd., Alto, MI 49302), and *Spirit Speaks* (The Kiowa

Foundation, P.O. Box 85400, Tucson, AZ 85754). The Internet provides a means of diffusing channeled texts at minimal cost to an audience currently numbering around 30 million and still growing exponentially. The UseNet discussion group alt.parapsychology.channeling receives new channeled material daily, as do discussion forums offered by Internet service-providers, including CompuServe and America Online. Momentum on the Internet has now moved to the graphically oriented World Wide Web, where new sites offering channeled texts, art, and even downloadable audio and video clips are appearing daily.

As one might expect, the spread of channeling has inspired a counter-literature critical of many forms of contemporary spiritualism. Books that claim to debunk channeling include Gordon, *Channeling into the New Age;* Alexander, *Spirit Channeling;* and Gardner, *The New Age.* For an account that evenhandedly assesses the rhetoric both of New Age texts and of the professional skeptics who disparage them, readers should consult Hess, *Science in the New Age.*

1. Into the Channeling Zone

1. This description is based on *Audience with Ramtha,* a set of two videotapes distributed by Ramtha Dialogues, Yelm, Washington, copyright 1986.

2. Melton et al., *New Age Encyclopedia,* xiii.

3. Sources on J. Z. Knight's 1992 alimony dispute include Timothy Egan, "Worldly and the Spiritual Clash in New Age Divorce," *New York Times,* September 25, 1992, A1; and Michael R. Dennett, "J. Z. Knight Divorce Trial Reveals Workings of Channeling Business," *Skeptical Inquirer* 17, no. 3 (1993):253–255. On the controversy over the use of federal monies for training programs provided by a disciple of J. Z. Knight, see Mark Hosenball, "The Guru and the FAA," *Newsweek,* March 6, 1995, 32. Since the late 1980s, the prophecies of Knight and Ramtha seem to have moved closer to those of right-wing survivalists and anti-Semites, who foresee a world held in the sinister grip of international bankers as part of a New World Order. See, for instance, Ramtha's pronouncements in Koteen, ed., *Last Waltz of the Tyrants.*

4. The definition of channeling proposed here closely parallels the formulation offered by Riordan in "Channeling: A New Revelation?" 105. Extensive definitional reflections are also found in Hastings, *With the Tongues of Men and Angels*; Klimo, *Channeling*; and Anderson, "Channeling." Authors who approach channeling from the perspective of parapsychology or transpersonal psychology have attempted to formulate a technical definition of channeling that distinguishes it from other altered states. As a social scientist, in contrast, I am interested in how people involved in channeling define what they do, regardless of whether their usage is consistent.

5. The estimate of the number of channels in Los Angeles is from Lynn Smith, "The New, Chic Metaphysical Fad of Channeling," *Los Angeles Times,* December 5, 1986, Section 5, 1. The Gallup survey data on belief in reincarnation and communication with the dead are reported in Leslie McAneny, "It Was a Very Bad Year: Belief in Hell and the Devil On Rise," *Gallup Organization Newsletter Archive* <http://www.gallup.com>, January 1995, unpaginated. The survey on belief in angels can be found in Nancy Gibbs, "Angels among Us," *Time,* December 27, 1993, 56–65. For estimates of spending on alternative medicine in the United States see Paul Trachtman, "NIH Looks at the Implausible and the Inexplicable," *Smithsonian,* September 1994, 110–123, and Mary Beth Regan, "Will a Cup of Cow's Whey Keep the Doctor Away?" *Business Week,* December 1994, 96.

6. D'Antonio, *Heaven on Earth,* 13. In contrast to the high figures reported by D'Antonio, a systematic telephone survey of American religious affiliation conducted by researchers at the City University of New York found that only about 20,000 Americans consider their religious affiliation to be "New Age." This observation is flawed, however, because most practitioners of New Age spirituality reject altogether the concept of religious affiliation and often object to the term "New Age." For details of the CUNY study, see Kosmin and Lachman, *One Nation under God.* The results of the CUNY study are accepted uncritically by Finke and Atark in their otherwise careful work *The Churching of America,*

1776–1990, leading them to the precipitous conclusion that the New Age "reflects interest levels on a par with reading astrology columns." Because the New Age is as much a sensibility as a social movement, research methods that attempt to measure its influence through such conventional indices as church membership will never grasp its full impact.

7. The primary sources for these demographic observations are the National Survey of Religious Identification (NSRI), summarized in Kosmin and Lachman, *One Nation under God,* and data presented in Roof, *A Generation of Seekers.* Interpretation of the NSRI survey is complicated by the authors' use of the term "New Age" as a religious affiliation. I have assumed that those who identified themselves as New Age have been folded into the authors' category of "New Religious Movements," the precise membership of which they do not clearly specify.

8. On Barbie channeling, see Anita Baskin, "The Spirit of Barbie," *Omni,* March 1994, 76. The source of the channeled conversation with Babe Ruth is Gerald A. Polley, "A Curve Ball from the Great Beyond," *Harper's Magazine,* February 1995, 31. See also Kathleen A. Hughes, "For Personal Insights, Some Try Channels Out of This World," *Wall Street Journal,* April 1, 1987, 1.

9. Ross, *Strange Weather,* 26–27. Other significant works on the New Age include Albanese, *Nature Religion in America;* Bednarowski, *New Religions and the Theological Imagination in American Culture;* Hess, *Science in the New Age;* Lewis and Melton, eds., *Perspectives on the New Age;* and Melton et al., *New Age Encyclopedia.* D'Antonio, a journalist, provides vivid accounts of a variety of New Age practices in *Heaven on Earth.* Other valuable case studies based on at least some participant-observation include Babbie, "Channels to Elsewhere"; Danforth, *Firewalking and Religious Healing;* English-Lueck, *Health in the New Age;* Hughes, "Blending with an Other; Luhrmann, *Persuasions of the Witch's Craft;* and Tipton, *Getting Saved from the Sixties.* Studies that foreground narcissistic tendencies in New Age thought and practice include Rossman, *New Age Blues;* Schapiro, "From Narcissism to the New Spiritualism"; and Shur, *The Awareness Trap.*

10. The past fifteen years have seen the near-collapse of scholarly consensus about whether one can say anything meaningful about "American religion" or even whether the United States has a shared national culture. For readers steadfastly committed to the idea that the United States consists of an increasingly centrifugal gathering of distinct cultures, I will specify that when I use the term "American" in this book I am principally talking about Euro-American or Anglo-American middle-class society, still the nation's dominant cultural influence. Although the majority of people involved in channeling are Euro-Americans, New Age religious practices are characterized as much as anything by their eclecticism, one expression of which is a willingness to incorporate influences from Native American, European, Asian, and African religions. For an elegant analysis of the philosophical implications of scholarly tribalism, see Geertz, "The Way We Think Now." An assessment of the influence of these developments on the study of American religions can be found in Sherrill, "Recovering American Religious Sensibility."

11. Lifton, *The Protean Self.*

2. Linking Up

1. Hughes and Melville, "Changes in Brainwave Activity During Trance Channeling."

2. Spiegel and Cardeña, "Disintegrated Experience," 367.

3. *Diagnostic and Statistical Manual of Mental Disorders (DSM-IV)*, 484. The *DSM-IV* describes a related condition called "dissociative disorder not otherwise specified" encompassing altered states in which patients "describe external spirits or entities that have entered their bodies and taken control," implying that channeling might qualify as a dissociative disorder. This theme is also addressed in Cardeña, "Trance and Possession as Dissociative Disorders."

4. The study comparing channels and patients with multiple personality is Hughes, "Differences between Trance Channeling and Multiple Personality Disorder on Structured Interview"; similar

clinical data with different comparison groups are reported in
Stifler et al., "An Empirical Investigation of the Discriminability
of Reported Mystical Experiences among Religious Contemplatives, Psychotic Inpatients, and Normal Adults." A comprehensive
overview of psychiatry's parallel interests in multiple personality
and communication with spirits is presented in Kenny, *The Passion
of Anselm Bourne;* see also his "Multiple Personality and Spirit Possession." An analysis that explicitly identifies channeling with multiple personality is Rogers, "Multiple Personality Disorder and
Channeling."

5. Even among sympathetic observers, the subtlety of the transformation raises questions about whether the channel's consciousness is
truly changed and, if so, how much. As Peters and Price-Williams
point out in a comparative analysis of shamanic trance, it is difficult
to assess the depth of trance even in societies that practice "classic" forms of shamanism. Some anthropologists have questioned
whether the shamans they have observed entered trance at all.
These cases are, of course, counterbalanced by instances where
shamans unquestionably achieve an altered state of consciousness
by means of trance-dancing or the ingestion of hallucinogenic sub-
stances. See Peters and Price-Williams, "Towards an Experiential
Analysis of Shamanism." Other works consulted for this discussion
include Winkelman, "Trance States," and Tart, "A Systems Approach to Altered States of Consciousness."

6. Hastings, *With the Tongues of Angels,* 152–154.

7. For general information on Theosophy, see Campbell, *Ancient
Wisdom Revived;* Cranston, *HPB;* and Ellwood and Partin, *Religious and Spiritual Groups in Modern America,* chap. 3.

8. The terminology used to describe these two poles of the channeling continuum varies widely. Trance channeling is sometimes
called "blending," "full-trance channeling," and "full-attunement
channeling." Alternative labels applied to conscious channeling include "light-trance channeling," "conscious, integrated channeling," and "open channeling." For details and debate, see Klimo,
Channeling; Hastings, *With the Tongues of Men and Angels;* and
Hughes, "Blending with an Other."

9. As Ryerson is a public figure in the New Age movement, I have felt free to use his real name. In any event, his style of channeling and the entities for whom he speaks are so distinctive that it would be impossible to maintain his anonymity. Details of the philosophical underpinnings of his work can be found in Ryerson and Harolde, *Spirit Communication.* For an uncompromisingly hostile view of Ryerson's approach to channeling, see Gardner, *The New Age.*

10. D'Antonio, *Heaven on Earth,* 208.

11. Debates about the virtues and liabilities of trance took place among nineteenth-century spiritualists as well. On the one hand, female mediums were allowed to speak before large crowds precisely because they had, in a sense, given themselves over to a higher (male) power. This prompted one prominent spiritualist, Mary Fenn Davis, to question the wisdom of abdicating the self through trance. According to the historian Ann Braude, Davis told an audience, "It is an abuse of Spiritualism to *yield up selfhood* in the absorbing investigation of the phenomena." See Braude, *Radical Spirits,* 89, 190.

12. Sarah Grey Thomason, the linguist who studied channeled speech, determined that the accents produced by channels were either erroneous (when they claimed to reproduce a known dialect) or inconsistent (for instance, when they were represented as the voice of extraterrestrials), leading her to conclude that the dialects were faked. Thomason's analysis is persuasive yet limited by her focus on debunking the truth-claims of channels. Using the same logic, one could also "debunk" the performances of spirit mediums in other societies without producing any insight into the cultural meaning of mediumship. My own less systematic study of channeled speech suggests that some channels are capable of spontaneous utterances remarkable for their fluidity and idiosyncratic syntax, although I agree with Thomason that the accents produced by channels are marked by inconsistency and, after long channeling sessions, near-collapse. See Thomason, "'Entities' in the Linguistic Minefield," and Roberts, "A Linguistic 'Nay' to Channeling."

13. The channels whom I interviewed or observed rarely considered the paradoxes of speech said to come from other worlds or dimen-

sions. An interesting exception was a Colorado-based channel who explained that English provides few resources for conveying "fifth-dimensional perspectives." A document distributed at his channeling session asserted that "the English language has evolved on this planet to support the male-dominant civilization that has existed here for thousands of years. As a result, right–wrong and hierarchy are implied by almost anything that is said in English."

14. Key sources on the Michael Teachings include Yarbro, *Messages from Michael,* and Stevens and Warwick-Smith, *The Michael Handbook.* There are at least ten other published books on various facets of the Michael Teachings. Regular reports on the Michael Teachings are found in *Michael's Progress,* a publication of the Michael Educational Foundation, 10 Muth Drive, Orinda, CA 94563.

15. John Payne, "Channeling—A Natural Skill Easily Learned," <http://www.spiritweb.org/Spirit/channeling-omni.html>, April 5, 1996, unpaginated.

3. Channeled Theology

1. The fliers were produced by David Stafford, P.O. Box 4823, Santa Fe, NM 87502, and are quoted with permission.

2. *SEDONA Journal of EMERGENCE!,* December 1993, 48.

3. The "Reverse Channeling Facilitator" was advertised in the *Federation Flash* 29, Spring 1995, an on-line magazine published by Starbuilders, an organization based in Hollywood, Florida.

4. See Hess, *Science in the New Age,* especially 85–93.

5. Harding, "After the Neutrality Idea," 568. Although Harding is a critic of objectivity, she also argues forcefully against relativism, which she dismisses as "objectivism's twin," in favor of "standpoint epistemology," which assumes that only those on the margins of the cultural mainstream are in a position to achieve relatively undistorted understandings (ibid., 583). The work of Harding and other critics of science is assessed in Gross and Levitt, *Higher Superstition.* Gross and Levitt seem to believe that New Age attitudes have infected the academic critics of science; I would

argue the reverse, although we agree that the two are part of a broad cultural process.

6. Writing about the social world of public-relations executives, the sociologist Robert Jackall quotes one executive to the effect that "Everyone out there is constructing reality." In the world of public relations, Jackall concludes, truth is "an irrelevant concept or one that is wholly kaleidoscopic . . . As long as a kind of plausibility is maintained, one perspective is as good as any other." See Jackall, *Moral Mazes,* 183.

7. *Revelations of Awareness,* no. 447, April 1995, an unpaginated on-line publication <http://www.tezcat.com/cosmic.awareness/html/cachome.html>.

8. Ryerson and Harolde, *Spirit Communication,* 97.

9. This discussion of common themes expressed in channeling draws on my own fieldwork as well as the following studies: Albanese, *Nature Religion in America;* Bednarowski, *New Religions and the Theological Imagination in American Culture;* Riordan, "Channeling"; and Babbie, "Channels to Elsewhere." The books by Albanese and Bednarowski are broad surveys of New Age theology, whereas Babbie and Riordan focus specifically on channeling.

10. An exception can be found in the Michael Teachings, which develop a systematic vision of the progress of the soul through multiple reincarnations. David and Sasha Johnson, the Michael channels introduced earlier, explained that everyone has an unchanging essence or basic personality that takes on a different "body personality" in each incarnation. As David put it, "The body has its own personality that's based on imprinting from the culture and the family." As souls develop, the basic personality emerges more strongly. What David called the "basic personality" or "essence" constitutes the true self that persists through multiple lifetimes. For a brief discussion of various versions of reincarnation and karma that have surfaced in Western spirituality, see Melton et al., *New Age Encyclopedia,* 384–390.

11. The curious history of the Hundredth Monkey story is reviewed in Clark, "Hundredth Monkey," and Amundson, "The Hundredth Monkey Debunked."

12. *Newsweek,* "Wheels of Misfortune," July 10, 1991, 28; see also James Bishop, Jr., "New Spirits of the Red Rocks," *Phoenix,* December 1990, 70–77. News reports mention that bewildered locals refer to the vortex tourists as "woo-woos" or "moon puppies." Although Sedona has what is probably considered the best collection of vortex sites in the country, other sacred sites that figure prominently in channeling practice include Mt. Shasta and the Tetons. For an informative history of the view that New Mexico has an intrinsically sacred and therapeutic landscape, see Fox, "Healing, Imagination, and New Mexico."

13. The principal sources consulted for this and subsequent discussions of American spiritualism are Braude, *Radical Spirits;* Hess, *Science in the New Age;* Moore, *In Search of White Crows;* Owen, *The Darkened Room;* and issues of two spiritualist publications, the *Spiritual Telegraph* and the *Shekinah,* both published in the 1850s. On contemporary spiritualism in the United States and England, see Nelson, *Spiritualism and Society;* Skultans, *Intimacy and Ritual;* and Zaretsky, "In the Beginning Was the Word." Information on Shaker spiritualism is from Anonymous, *A Revelation of the Extraordinary Visitation of Departed Spirits,* 1869. I owe this and subsequent references to Shaker material to Sylvia Kennick Brown, the Williams College archivist.

14. Channing, "The New Church," 50.

15. Courtney, "Cause and Cure of Crime," 84, and the *Spiritual Telegraph,* vol. 3 (1854): 175. Theosophy's role in transforming spiritualism from a popular to an elite movement is analyzed in Prothero, "From Spiritualism to Theosophy"; see also Moore, *In Search of White Crows,* 80–81 and 228.

16. Meyer, *The Positive Thinkers,* 35. See also Sir George Pickering, *Creative Malady.*

17. The A. B. Child passage is quoted in Moore, *In Search of White Crows,* 58. The statements by Davis are from his book *The Approaching Crisis,* 116. Courtney's remarks on the relationship between morality and deviance are from "Cause and Cure of Crime," 88.

18. I was accompanied to this event by David Hess and Emily Mar-

tin, whose comments afterwards have doubtless influenced my interpretation.

19. This issue is outlined with great clarity in Riordan, "Channeling," 118–121. Channeling's moral relativism is hardly unique in the world of post-1960s alternative spirituality and motivational training. For a perceptive analysis of the moral framework of the Erhard Seminars Training and other alternative religious or quasi-religious groups, see Tipton, *Getting Saved from the Sixties*. An interesting exception to New Age moral relativism is the Church Universal and Triumphant (CUT), whose teachings are based on revelations channeled by Mark Prophet and, after his death in 1973, by Elizabeth Claire Prophet. Apparently CUT enforces strict rules of personal morality similar to those of some evangelical Christian denominations.

20. Alleged victim-blaming in channeled teachings is discussed in Gardner, *The New Age*, and Henry Gordon, *Channeling into the New Age*. In *Illness as Metaphor*, Susan Sontag attempted to dispose of the argument that people somehow cause their own cancer, but it has now firmly established itself as orthodoxy in American alternative healing.

21. Wendy Kaminer offers a portrait of the current American obsession with victimhood in *I'm Dysfunctional, You're Dysfunctional*. While acknowledging that New Age thought offers an alternative to the celebration of victim status, Kaminer finds in it only mindless optimism and a cult of self-realization that fails to advocate meaningful social change. For a more thorough and dispassionate examination of self-help groups, see Wuthnow, *Sharing the Journey*.

22. Evans-Pritchard, *Witchcraft, Oracles, and Magic among the Azande*, 21.

23. Roof, *A Generation of Seekers*, 96 and 185–186.

4. Mastering Self-Expansion

1. In her discussion of shamanism, Deborah O'Neill specifically referred to Harner's *The Way of the Shaman*, a work that has proved influential in the development of New Age shamanism, or as it is sometimes called, neo-shamanism. Harner left a successful career

as an academic anthropologist to establish the Foundation for Shamanic Studies, located in Mill Valley, California.

2. More detailed discussions of Aguaruna shamanism can be found in Brown, "Shamanism and its Discontents" and "Dark Side of the Shaman." For an assessment of the semantically rich lyrics of healing songs elsewhere in Amazonia, see Hill, "A Musical Aesthetic of Ritual Curing in the Northwest Amazon."

3. Lewis, "What Is a Shaman?" 32. In response to Lewis's proposed redefinition, Erika Bourguignon has argued that there is a profound difference between actively seeking spiritual contact and passively receiving it. She coins the terms "visionary trancer" and "possession trancer" to distinguish between active and passive spiritual communication. For discussion, see Bourguignon, "Trance and Shamanism."

4. My source on the performances of Chico Xavier is Hess, *Samba in the Night.* See also Bastide, *The African Religions of Brazil,* and Press, "The Urban Curandero."

5. This discussion of Ndembu divination is based on Turner, *The Drums of Affliction.*

6. Taylor, *Sources of the Self,* 507.

7. See Roof, *A Generation of Seekers,* especially chap. 6.

5. Spiritual Androgyny

1. A 1994 conference exploring women-centered theology caused an uproar among conservative Methodists and Presbyterians, who strongly objected to the involvement of their churches in a meeting that they characterized as a celebration of goddess-worship. For details, see Peter Steinfels, "Female Concept of God is Shaking Protestants," *New York Times,* May 14, 1994, A8.

2. Works that document the influence—sometimes overt, sometimes subtle—of feminism on mainstream Christian denominations in the United States include Davie, *Women in the Presence;* Lenz and Myerhoff, *The Feminization of America;* and Stacey, *Brave New Families.* On the Promise Keepers, see Wagenheim, "Among the Promise Keepers." Key sources on the intersection between fem-

inism and alternative spirituality include Bednarowski, "The New Age Movement and Feminist Spirituality"; Griffin, "The Embodied Goddess"; Jacobs, "Women-Centered Healing Rites" and "Gender and Power in New Religious Movements"; Tanya M. Luhrmann, "The Resurgence of Romanticism"; Neitz, "In Goddess We Trust"; and Palmer, "Women's 'Cocoon Work' in New Religious Movements." A major comparative work on the status of women in new religious movements is Palmer, *Moon Sisters, Krishna Mothers, Rajneesh Lovers.* For an assessment of the status of women in traditional spiritualist congregations, see Haywood, "The Authority and Empowerment of Women among Spiritualist Groups."

3. Details of the life of Achsa Sprague are from Braude, *Radical Spirits.* On Annie Fairlamb, see Owen, *The Darkened Room.* A detailed historical analysis of sexual norms and the status of women in several utopian communities in the United States can be found in Kitch, *Chaste Liberation.*

4. The higher representation of women among therapeutic practitioners is to some extent a reflection of the feminization of psychotherapy since the 1970s; for details, see Philipson, *On the Shoulders of Women.* My data on the sex ratio of channels differ from those of Dureen Hughes, who reports rough parity between men and women in her sample of trance channels in the Los Angeles area. (See Hughes, "Blending with an Other," 179.) A recent survey published in the Winter 1994 issue of *Reality Change,* a magazine devoted to material channeled by Jane Roberts, reported that 67 percent of its readers were female. A surprising 44 percent of readers were age 55 or older; these may represent people who discovered Roberts's books when they were first published in the early 1970s. *Reality Change* is a publication of Seth Network International, P.O. Box 1620, Eugene, OR 97440.

5. The split-brain theory is now universally accepted among people involved in alternative spirituality. For a brief summary, see Ferguson, *The Aquarian Conspiracy,* 77–79.

6. Kaminer, "Feminism's Identity Crisis."

7. This description is based on the video *The Co-Creation of Heaven*

on Earth, produced by the Extraterrestrial Earth Mission, Sedona, Arizona, copyright 1987. On the tape, the three channels are identified only as Aktivar, Akria, and Akrista.

8. This analysis of the "I AM"'s Americanization of Theosophy is based on Ellwood and Partin, *Religious and Spiritual Groups in Modern America,* 98–102, and Braden, *These Also Believe,* 257–307. I have also consulted the useful biography of Guy Ballard in Melton et al., *New Age Encyclopedia,* as well as the bibliographic survey of the "I AM" Religious Activity and its offshoots in Bjorling, *Channeling.* For a summary of the Supreme Court's decisions on the "I AM" Activity, see Pfeffer, "The Legitimation of Marginal Religions in the United States," 20–24.

9. Lambek, *Human Spirits,* 76–79. Other important sources on the gendered quality of spirit possession include Lewis, *Ecstatic Religion,* and Boddy, *Wombs and Alien Spirits.*

10. Luhrmann, "The Resurgence of Romanticism," 229.

11. Parallels between this outlook and that of some male transvestites, who hold that cross-dressing is a path to achieving "the unification of self, the complete human being," are explored in Woodhouse, *Fantastic Women,* 84.

12. Boddy, *Wombs and Alien Spirits,* 351. On the constitution of gender through everyday performance, see Butler, *Gender Trouble.*

6. Dreaming of Community

1. Similar observations about the distinction between religion and spirituality among Baby Boomers can be found in Roof, *A Generation of Seekers,* 76–79.

2. *Spiritual Telegraph,* New Series, 3 (1854): 56, 477.

3. Although there is far more skepticism about prospects for life in communes today than there was in the 1970s, small intentional communities—many organized according to New Age principles—still dot the landscape of the United States. Prominent examples include the Sirius Community in Massachusetts and Sparrow Hawk Village in Oklahoma. For a comprehensive survey of such communities, see McLaughlin and Davidson, *Builders of the Dawn.*

4. Kelly, "Embrace It," 24. Other works exploring links between New Age rhetoric and dreams of virtual reality include Davis, "Techgnosis," and Hayward, "Situating Cyberspace." On the prospects for electronic community, see Rheingold, *The Virtual Community;* on its questionable reality, Jones, "Understanding Community in the Information Age," and Talbott, *The Future Does Not Compute.*

5. Katz, "Return of the Luddites," 210.

6. Turkle, *Life on the Screen,* 244.

7. Sources on the tangled history of the "I AM" Religious Activity and the Church Universal and Triumphant include Melton et al., *New Age Encyclopedia,* 57–60 and 361–362; and Ellwood and Partin, *Religious and Spiritual Groups in Modern America,* 102–106. Journalistic accounts describing the controversies surrounding CUT's activities in Montana include "The Cloud over Paradise Valley," *People,* June 4, 1990, 48–53; Michael Hirsley, "Leader of A Cult? No, She Insists," *Chicago Tribune,* March 3 1993, C-2.; Ann Japenga, "A Test of Faith," *Los Angeles Times,* March 29, 1990, E-1; Holger Jensen, "Trouble in Paradise," *Maclean's,* May 7, 1990, 33–35; and the *New York Times,* "Group Gives Up Weapons for Tax Exemption," June 5, 1994, A-31.

Stories about other alleged channeling cults continue to appear in the local and national media. In 1993, for example, the *Virginian-Pilot* of Norfolk, Virginia, published a page-one story about two channels who allegedly bilked thirty followers out of their personal savings and induced them to perform public sex acts (Cody Lowe, "Saying They Gave Body and Mind, Ex-churchgoers Sue 'Masters'," *Virginian-Pilot,* May 4, 1993, A-1). More recently, a series of accidental deaths in northern New Mexico prompted front-page stories about a group called The Genesis Alliance, whose leaders claim to be walk-ins, humans whose bodies have been taken over by extraterrestrials. For details, see Mark Oswald and Steve Terrell, "Fatal Falls Stir Questions about Group," *Sante Fe New Mexican,* April 10, 1994, A-1.

8. Klaw, *Without Sin*, 221. Noyes vacillated in his attitude toward the independent spiritualist explorations of community members,

sometimes supporting them, sometimes expressing doubts about their validity. For discussion of the tensions between authoritarianism and radical individualism in spiritualist communities, see Carroll, "Spiritualism and Community in Antebellum America."

9. Galanter, *Cults, Faith, Healing, and Coercion,* 197–199.

10. The names of the two congregations described in the following discussion are pseudonyms.

11. For a comparative analysis of spiritualist services elsewhere, see Zaretsky, "In the Beginning was the Word."

12. Melton et al., *New Age Encyclopedia,* 8–9.

13. Data on trends in American religious affiliation are from Finke and Rodney, *The Churching of America.* On declining church attendance and its possible significance, see Putnam, "Bowling Alone."

14. This reflects the consumerist attitude of Baby Boomers who return to organized religion after a period of withdrawal: "A psychological language of 'choices' and 'needs' replaces older-style religious obligations as a basis for getting involved in a congregation" (Roof, *A Generation of Seekers,* 192). For additional data on "religious shopping," see Kosmin and Lachman, *One Nation under God.*

15. Bellah et al., *Habits of the Heart,* especially chap. 5. The concept of the therapeutic society was first developed in Rieff's influential book *The Triumph of the Therapeutic.*

16. Putnam, "Bowling Alone."

17. Wuthnow, *Sharing the Journey,* especially 1–58.

7. Spiritual Commerce

1. Root, *Cannibal Culture,* 88. See also Gardner, *The New Age,* who coined the term "trance chiseling" for J. Z. Knight's alleged practice of extorting large fees from her clients.

2. McLoughlin, *Revivals, Awakenings, and Reform,* 28. For an engaging history of religion and money in America, see Moore, *Selling God.* The money-making practices of new religious movements are analyzed in Richardson, ed., *Money and Power in the New Religions.*

3. Wuthnow, *Meaning and Moral Order,* 88.

4. Ferguson, *The Aquarian Conspiracy.* Ironically, Ferguson's book

was so successful that a publisher reportedly paid her a six-figure royalty advance for her next.

5. Writing around 1900, the German sociologist Georg Simmel noted money's "indifferent and empty character." Because money allows us to establish universal equivalences, Simmel argued, "things submit more and more defenselessly to the power of money" (Simmel, *The Philosophy of Money,* 232–233). Other works on the cross-cultural significance of money consulted for this discussion include Taussig, *The Devil and Commodity Fetishism in South America;* Parry and Bloch, "Introduction: Money and the Morality of Exchange"; and Hillman, "A Contribution to Soul and Money."

6. McLaughlin and Davidson, *Builders of the Dawn,* 148–149. The view that money is an infinitely abundant element has, in fact, been around for at least a century. In 1904, for example, Elizabeth Towne published *Practical Methods for Self-Development,* in which she states that "money is really as free as air." (Towne's work is quoted in Griswold, "New Thought," 315.) The philosophical implications of the modern dematerialization of money are analyzed by Mark C. Taylor in *Disfiguring: Art, Architecture, Religion,* chap. 5.

7. For brief histories of New Thought and prosperity consciousness, see Melton et al., *New Age Encyclopedia,* 326–331 and 362–366, as well as Griswold's, "New Thought." Sources on the links between New Thought and American business include Rupert, "Employing the New Age"; Bromley and Shupe, "Rebottling the Elixir"; and Greil and Robbins, "Introduction: Exploring the Boundaries of the Sacred."

8. Marashansky, "Bankruptcy," *New Visions* (Pittsfield, Mass.), Summer 1993, 5. Other sources on prosperity consciousness are Martin, "Health and Wealth in the U.S.A.," and Dahl, *Beyond the Winning Streak: Using Conscious Creation to Consistently Win at Life.*

9. The term "emotional work" comes from Arlie Russell Hochschild, *The Managed Heart,* a book that focuses specifically on the case of flight attendants as a pivotal example of the difficulties of such labor. For additional reflections on questions of emotional authenticity in the workplace, see Bellah et al., *Habits of the Heart,* 123–125, and Oakes, *The Soul of the Salesman.*

10. The workshops I document here seem to have been influenced in varying degrees by Erhard Seminars Training *(est)*, a group that during its heyday in the 1970s combined the insights of the personal-growth movement and techniques of prosperity consciousness to produce an influential quasi-religious philosophy of success. "According to *est*'s ethic, the individual's felt well-being follows from his having a life that works, which follows from his setting goals and achieving them," writes Steven M. Tipton. "Achievement follows from self-acceptance, that is, feeling good about oneself." See Tipton, *Getting Saved from the Sixties,* 211, as well as Abraham, "The Protestant Ethic and the Spirit of Utilitarianism." For discussion of the controversy about whether motivational training produces verifiable results, see Lemann, "Is There a Science of Success?"

11. D'Antonio, *Heaven on Earth,* 133.

12. See Royal Ford, "Putting Pricetags on a Culture," *Boston Sunday Globe,* March 14. 1993, A-41, and Smith, "For All Those Who Were Indian in a Former Life." Additional sources on the alleged appropriation of Native spirituality by non-Indians involved in New Age spirituality include "Indians Express Contempt for Wanna-be Tribes, Ceremonies," *Santa Fe New Mexican,* September 3, 1993, A-6; Churchill, "Sam Gill's Mother Earth"; Glass-Coffin, "Anthropology, Shamanism, and the 'New Age'"; Kehoe, "Prima Gaia"; Root, *Cannibal Culture;* and Rose, "The Great Pretenders." An admirably evenhanded account of the influence of Native American thought on American alternative spirituality is Albanese, *Nature Religion in America.*

13. Sedona, Arizona, has been the epicenter of a series of conflicts between practitioners of New Age religion and the U.S. Forest Service over the proper use of public lands that New Agers believe contain energy vortexes. Various Indian tribes have also registered protests over the alleged desecration of sacred sites on these lands. For details of the Sedona controversy, see Mary Tolan, "Time Bandits: Vandals Destroying Archaeological Sites," *Arizona Daily Sun,* (Flagstaff, Ariz.), November 12, 1994, 1, and James Bishop, Jr., "New Spirits of the Red Rocks," *Phoenix,* December 1990,

70–77. (My thanks to Peter J. Pilles, Jr., Forest Archaeologist of the Coconino National Forest, for these materials.) Encounters between Latin American Indians and New Age tourists are analyzed in Schaefer, "Huichols, the New Age Movement, and the Native American Church;" Fikes, *Carlos Castaneda, Academic Opportunism, and the Psychedelic Sixties;* and Joralemon, "The Selling of the Shaman and the Problem of Informant Legitimacy."

14. The description of Indian visits to Shaker communities is from the Williams College Archives and Special Collections, Shaker Collection 98, vol. 4, no. 44. On William James, Lenora Piper, and Chlorine, see Kenny, *The Passion of Anselm Bourne,* 113.

15. See, for instance, Root, *Cannibal Culture,* 78–81.

16. A detailed analysis of the Zuni repatriation claim is presented in Merrill et al., "The Return of the *Ahayu:da.*" Zuni Pueblo's request for the return of religious images and associated articles was approved on legal grounds relating to the uncertainty of the Smithsonian Institution's legal title, not on the sweeping notion of intellectual property asserted by the Zunis.

17. Noting the tendency of religion to become a commodity in modern, pluralist societies, James Davison Hunter observes that Christian evangelicalism has increasingly become "packaged for easy, rapid, and strain-free consumption." See *American Evangelicalism*, 84.

18. The number of degree programs in clinical psychology approved by the American Psychological Association, for instance, increased sevenfold between 1948 and 1989, and the number of licensed psychologists more than doubled between 1975 and 1985; for details, see Nietzel et al., *Introduction to Clinical Psychology,* 29, and Manderscheid and Sonnenschein, eds., *Mental Health, United States 1990,* 199. At the master's level, there was more than a threefold increase in the number of degrees awarded between 1966 and 1990 (American Psychological Association, personal communication). Information on growth in psychotherapy's unregulated, informal sector is difficult to obtain, but presumably it constitutes a significant portion of the billions spent on alternative healing in the United States each year.

19. For a medical assessment of the effectiveness of non-Western therapeutic practices in psychotherapeutic settings, see Zatzick and Johnson, "Indigenous Psychotherapeutic Practices among Middle Class Americans: I," and Johnson and Zatzick, "Indigenous Psychotherapeutic Practices among Middle Class Americans: II." The use of channeling in nursing practice is assessed by Nancy Doyne in her essay "Channeling and Other Esoteric Methods of Self-Care."

20. Ellwood, *Alternative Altars,* 33. For a comprehensive history of the links between new religions and alternative therapies, see Fuller, *Alternative Medicine and American Religious Life.*

8. Being Multiple

1. Tocqueville, *Democracy in America,* 429. The role of the entrepreneurial spirit in the rise of new religions is explored by Zaretsky and Leone in the introduction to their valuable compendium *Religious Movements in Contemporary America.*

2. Lifton, *The Protean Self,* 5, 9. See also Giddens, *Modernity and Self-Identity,* and Gergen, *The Saturated Self.*

3. Turkle, *Life on the Screen,* 14, 24.

4. For additional reflections on parallels between new media and religious thought, see Davis, "Techgnosis," and Taylor and Saarinen, *Imagologies.*

5. Braude, *Radical Spirits,* 40–41, 53.

6. Ross, "Epidemiology of Multiple Personality Disorder and Dissociation," 506.

7. Hacking, *Rewriting the Soul,* 236. For discussion of the epidemiology and symptoms of multiple personality, see Ross, "Epidemiology of Multiple Personality Disorder and Dissociation" and "Twelve Cognitive Errors about Multiple Personality Disorder." Skeptical assessments of multiple personality include Merskey, "The Manufacture of Personalities"; Nathan, "Dividing to Conquer?"; and Spanos et al., "Multiple Personality."

8. Braun, "Issues in the Psychotherapy of Multiple Personality Disorder," 15. For advocacy and self-help written by self-identified multiples, see Lynn W., ed., *Mending Ourselves,* and "Dissociation:

An Informal Look from an Insider," the Frequently Asked Question (FAQ) document from the UseNet newsgroup alt.support.dissociation, downloaded November 19, 1995. Psychological contrasts between channels and multiples are assessed in Hughes, "Differences between Trance Channeling and Multiple Personality Disorder on Structured Interview."

9. Haaken, "Sexual Abuse, Recovered Memory, and Therapeutic Practice," 134, 136.

10. Belief that society and culture function largely to repress individuals and to limit the realization of their full potential is a prominent theme in a number of "quasi-religious" therapeutic movements in the United States, including Scientology, Lifespring, and Erhard Seminars Training. For details and analysis, see Adams and Haaken, "Anticultural Culture," and Robbins and Bromley, "What Have We Learned about New Religions?"

11. Lewis H. Lapham, "Seen But Not Heard: The Message of the Oklahoma Bombings," *Harper's Magazine,* July 1995, 29–36.

12. On new religions in the United States see Melton, "Another Look at New Religions," and Robbins and Bromley, "What Have We Learned about New Religions?"

13. The online statement, which is quoted with the kind permission of Glenda M. Stocks, was posted in the UseNet discussion group alt.paranormal.channeling on June 10, 1994. Sources on millenarian tendencies in Western culture include Schwartz, *Century's End,* and Boyer, *When Time Shall Be No More.*

14. See Melton, "New Thought and the New Age," 29. Although my discussion has focused solely on channeling's trajectory in the United States, American channels or movements based on their teachings have succeeded in establishing footholds in some European countries, as well as in New Zealand. Studies of the impact of channeling and other New Age practices outside of the United States can be found in Ellwood, *Islands of the Dawn;* Lewis and Melton, eds., *Perspectives on the New Age;* and Stark, "Europe's Receptivity to New Religious Movements."

15. Huizinga, *Homo Ludens,* 28. See also Handelman, *Models and Mirrors*, especially chap. 3.

BIBLIOGRAPHY

Abraham, Gary. "The Protestant Ethic and the Spirit of Utilitarianism: The Case of EST." *Theory and Society* 12 (1983): 739–73.

Adams, Richard, and Janice Haaken. "Anticultural Culture: Lifespring's Ideology and Its Roots in Humanistic Psychology." *Journal of Humanistic Psychology* 27, no. 4 (1987).

Albanese, Catherine L. *Nature Religion in America: From the Algonkian Indians to the New Age.* Chicago, Ill.: University of Chicago Press, 1990.

Alexander, Brooks. *Spirit Channeling: Evaluating the Latest in New Age Spiritism.* Downers Grove, Ill.: InterVarsity Press, 1988.

Amundson, Ron. "The Hundredth Monkey Debunked." *The Whole Earth Review* 52 (1986): 19–25.

Anderson, Rodger. "Channeling." *Parapsychology Review* 15, no. 5 (1988): 6–9.

Andrews, Ted. *How to Meet and Work with Spirit Guides.* St. Paul, Minn.: Llewellyn Publications, 1992.

Anonymous. *A Revelation of the Extraordinary Visitation of Departed Spirits of Distinguished Men and Women of All Nations and Their Manifestation through the Living Bodies of the "Shakers."* Philadelphia, Pa.: L. G. Thomas, 1869. Shaker Collection, Williams College Archives and Special Collections.

Babbie, Earl. "Channels to Elsewhere." In *In Gods We Trust: New Patterns of Religious Pluralism in America,* 2nd rev. ed., edited by Thomas Robbins and Dick Anthony, 255–68. New Brunswick, N.J.: Transaction Publishers, 1990.

Bastide, Roger. *The African Religions of Brazil: Toward a Sociology of the Interpenetration of Civilizations.* Translated by Helen Sebba. Baltimore, Md.: Johns Hopkins University Press, 1978 [orig. 1960].

Bednarowski, Mary Farrell. *New Religions and the Theological Imagination in American Culture.* Bloomington, Ind.: Indiana University Press, 1989.

———. "The New Age Movement and Feminist Spirituality: Overlapping Conversations at the End of the Century." In *Perspectives on the New Age,* edited by James R. Lewis and J. Gordon Melton, 167–78. Albany, N.Y.: State University of New York Press, 1992.

Bellah, Robert N., Richard Madsen, William M. Sullivan, Ann Swidler, and Steven M. Tipton. *Habits of the Heart: Individualism and Commitment in American Life.* New York: Harper & Row/Perennial, 1985.

Bjorling, Joel. *Channeling: A Bibliographic Exploration.* Sects and Cults in America, Bibliographic Guide No. 15. New York: Garland Publishing, 1992.

Boddy, Janice Patricia. *Wombs and Alien Spirits: Women, Men, and the Zar Cult in Northern Sudan.* Madison, Wis.: University of Wisconsin Press, 1989.

Bourguignon, Erika. "Trance and Shamanism: What's in a Name?" *Journal of Psychoactive Drugs* 21, no. 1 (1989): 9–15.

Boyer, Paul. *When Time Shall Be No More: Prophecy Beliefs in Modern American Culture.* Cambridge, Mass.: Harvard University Press, 1992.

Braden, Charles Samuel. *These Also Believe: A Study of Modern American Cults and Minority Religious Movements.* New York: Macmillan, 1956.

Braude, Ann. *Radical Spirits: Spiritualism and Women's Rights in Nineteenth-Century America.* Boston: Beacon Press, 1989.

Braun, Bennett G. "Issues in the Psychotherapy of Multiple Personality Disorder." In *Treatment of Multiple Personality Disorder,* edited by Bennett G. Braun, 3–28. Washington, D.C.: American Psychiatric Press, 1986.

Bromley, David G., and Anson Shupe. "Rebottling the Elixir: The

Gospel of Prosperity in America's Religioeconomic Corporations." In *In Gods We Trust: New Patterns of Religious Pluralism in
America,* 2nd rev. ed., edited by Thomas Robbins and Dick Anthony, 233–54. New Brunswick, N.J.: Transaction Publishers,
1990.

Brown, Michael F. "Dark Side of the Shaman." *Natural History,* November 1989, 8–10.

————. "Shamanism and Its Discontents." *Medical Anthropology Quarterly* 2, no. 2 (1988): 102–20.

Butler, Judith. *Gender Trouble: Feminism and the Subversion of Identity.*
London: Routledge, 1990.

Campbell, Bruce F. *Ancient Wisdom Revived: A History of the Theosophical Movement.* Berkeley: University of California Press, 1980.

Cardeña, Etzel. "Trance and Possession as Dissociative Disorders."
Transcultural Psychiatric Research Review 29 (1992): 287–300.

Carroll, Bret E. "Spiritualism and Community in Antebellum America: The Mountain Cove Episode." *Communal Societies* 12 (1992):
20–39.

Channing, William C. "The New Church." *Spiritual Telegraph* 3
(1854): 42–50.

Churchill, Ward. "Sam Gill's *Mother Earth:* Colonialism, Genocide
and the Expropriation of Indigenous Spiritual Tradition in Contemporary Academia." *American Indian Culture and Research Journal* 12, no. 3 (1988): 49–67.

Clark, Jerome. "Hundredth Monkey." In *New Age Encyclopedia,* J.
Gordon Melton et al., 225–27. Detroit, Mich.: Gale Research,
1990.

A Course in Miracles. Tiburon, Cal.: Foundation for Inner Peace, 1975.

Courtney, W. S. "Cause and Cure of Crime, No. III." *Spiritual Telegraph* 3 (1854): 81–90.

Cranston, Sylvia L. *HPB: The Extraordinary Life and Influence of Helena
Blavatsky, Founder of the Modern Theosophical Movement.* New
York: F. P. Putnam's Sons, 1994.

Dahl, Lynda Madden. *Beyond the Winning Streak: Using Conscious Creation to Consistently Win at Life.* Eugene, Ore.: Windsong Publishing, 1993.

Danforth, Loring M. *Firewalking and Religious Healing: The Anastenaria of Greece and the American Firewalking Movement*. Princeton, N.J.: Princeton University Press, 1989.

Davie, Jody Shapiro. *Women in the Presence: Constructing Community and Seeking Spirituality in Mainline Protestantism*. Philadelphia: University of Pennsylvania Press, 1995.

Davis, Andrew Jackson. *The Approaching Crisis, Being a Review of Dr. Bushnell's Course of Lectures on the Bible, Nature, Religion, Skepticism, and the Supernatural*, 4th ed. Boston: William White and Co., 1873.

Davis, Erik. "Techgnosis: Magic, Memory and the Angels of Information." In *Flame Wars: The Discourse of Cyberculture*, edited by Mark Dery, 585–616. Special Issue of *South Atlantic Quarterly*, Vol. 92, 1993.

Doyne, Nancy. "Channeling and Other Esoteric Methods of Self-Care." *Holistic Nursing Practice* 4, no. 4 (1990): 70–76.

DSM-IV. *Diagnostic and Statistical Manual of Mental Disorders, Fourth Edition*. Washington, D.C.: American Psychiatric Association, 1994.

D'Antonio, Michael. *Heaven on Earth: Dispatches from America's Spiritual Frontier*. New York: Crown Publishers, 1992.

Ellwood, Robert S. *Alternative Altars: Unconventional and Eastern Spirituality in America*. Chicago: University of Chicago Press, 1979.

———. *Islands of the Dawn: The Story of Alternative Spirituality in New Zealand*. Honolulu: University of Hawaii Press, 1993.

———, and Harry B. Partin. *Religious and Spiritual Groups in Modern America*, 2nd ed. Englewood Cliffs, N.J.: Prentice Hall, 1988.

English-Lueck, J. A. *Health in the New Age: A Study of California Holistic Practices*. Albuquerque, N.M.: University of New Mexico Press, 1990.

Ferguson, Marilyn. *The Aquarian Conspiracy: Personal and Social Transformation in Our Time*. Los Angeles: Tarcher, 1980.

Fikes, Jay Courtney. *Carlos Castaneda, Academic Opportunism and the Psychedelic Sixties*. Victoria, B.C.: Millenia Press, 1993.

Finke, Roger, and Rodney Stark. *The Churching of America, 1776–1990: Winners and Losers in Our Religious Economy*. New Brunswick, N.J.: Rutgers University Press, 1992.

Fox, Stephen D. "Healing, Imagination, and New Mexico." *New Mexico Historical Review* 58, no. 3 (1983): 213–37.

Fuller, Robert C. *Alternative Medicine and American Religious Life*. New York: Oxford University Press, 1989.

Galanter, Marc. *Cults, Faith, Healing, and Coercion*. New York: Oxford University Press, 1989.

Gardner, Martin. *The New Age: Notes of a Fringe Watcher*. Buffalo, N.Y.: Prometheus Books, 1988.

Geertz, Clifford. "The Way We Think Now: Toward an Ethnography of Modern Thought." In *Local Knowledge: Further Essays in Interpretive Anthropology*, 147–66. New York: Basic Books, 1983.

Gergen, Kenneth J. *The Saturated Self: Dilemmas of Identity in Contemporary Life*. New York: Basic Books, 1991.

Giddens, Anthony. *Modernity and Self-Identity: Self and Society in the Late Modern Age*. Stanford, Cal.: Stanford University Press, 1991.

Glass-Coffin, Bonnie. "Anthropology, Shamanism, and the 'New Age.'" *Chronicle of Higher Education*, June 15, 1994, A48.

Gordon, Henry. *Channeling Into the New Age: The "Teachings" of Shirley MacLaine and Other Such Gurus*. Buffalo, N.Y.: Prometheus Books, 1988.

Greil, Arthur L., and Thomas Robbins. "Introduction: Exploring the Boundaries of the Sacred." In *Between Sacred and Secular*, edited by Arthur L. Greil and Thomas Robbins, 1–23. Religion and the Social Order, no. 4. Greenwich, Conn: JAI Press, 1994.

Griffin, Wendy. "The Embodied Goddess: Feminist Witchcraft and Female Divinity." *Sociology of Religion* 56, no. 1 (1995): 35–48.

Griswold, Alfred W. "New Thought: A Cult of Success." *American Journal of Sociology* 40 (1934): 309–18.

Groothius, Douglas R. *Unmasking the New Age*. Downers Grove, Ill.: InterVarsity Press, 1986.

Gross, Paul R., and Norman Levitt. *Higher Superstition: The Academic Left and Its Quarrels with Science*. Baltimore, Md.: Johns Hopkins University Press, 1994.

Haaken, Janice. "Sexual Abuse, Recovered Memory, and Therapeutic Practice: A Feminist-Psychoanalytic Perspective." *Social Text* 40 (Fall 1994): 115–45.

Hacking, Ian. *Rewriting the Soul: Multiple Personality and the Sciences of Memory*. Princeton, N.J.: Princeton University Press, 1995.

Handelman, Don. *Models and Mirrors: Towards an Anthropology of Public Events*. Cambridge: Cambridge University Press, 1990.

Harding, Sandra. "After the Neutrality Ideal: Science, Politics, and 'Strong Objectivity.'" *Social Research* 59 (1992): 567–87.

Harding, Susan F. "Convicted by the Holy Spirit: The Rhetoric of Fundamental Baptist Conversion." *American Ethnologist* 14, no. 1 (1987): 167–81.

Harner, Michael J. *The Way of the Shaman: A Guide to Power and Healing*. San Francisco, Cal: Harper and Row, 1980.

Hastings, Arthur. *With the Tongues of Men and Angels: A Study of Channeling*. Henry Rolfs Book Series, Institute of Noetic Sciences. Fort Worth, Tex.: Holt, Rinehart and Winston, 1991.

Hayward, Philip. "Situating Cyberspace: The Popularisation of Virtual Reality." In *Future Visions: New Technologies of the Screen,* edited by Philip Hayward and Tana Wollen, 180–204. London: Arts Council of Great Britain & BFI Publishing, 1993.

Haywood, Carol Lois. "The Authority and Empowerment of Women among Spiritualist Groups." *Journal for the Scientific Study of Religion* 22, no. 2 (1983): 157–66.

Hess, David J. *Science in the New Age: The Paranormal, Its Defenders and Debunkers, and American Culture*. Madison, Wis.: University of Wisconsin Press, 1993.

———. *Samba in the Night: Spiritism in Brazil*. New York: Columbia University Press, 1994.

Hexham, Irving. "The Evangelical Response to the New Age." In *Perspectives on the New Age,* edited by James R. Lewis and J. Gordon Melton, 152–64. Albany, N.Y.: State University of New York Press, 1992.

Hill, Jonathan D. "A Musical Aesthetic of Ritual Curing in the Northwest Amazon." In *Portals of Power: Shamanism in South America,* edited by E. Jean Matteson Langdon, 175–210. Albuquerque, N.M.: University of New Mexico Press, 1992.

Hill, Napoleon. *Think and Grow Rich*. New York: Fawcett Crest, 1960 [orig. 1937].

Hillman, James. "A Contribution to Soul and Money." In *Soul and Money,* Proceedings of the 8th International Congress of the International Association for Analytical Psychology, 31–44. Dallas, Tex.: Spring Publications, 1982.

Hochschild, Arlie Russell. *The Managed Heart: Commercialization of Human Feelings.* Berkeley: University of California Press, 1983.

Hughes, Dureen J. "Blending with an Other: An Analysis of Trance Channeling in the United States." *Ethos* 19, no. 2 (1991): 161–84.

———. "Differences Between Trance Channeling and Multiple Personality Disorder on Structured Interview." *Journal of Transpersonal Psychology* 24, no. 2 (1992): 181–92.

———, and Norbert T. Melville. "Changes in Brainwave Activity During Trance Channeling: A Pilot Study." *Journal of Transpersonal Psychology* 22, no. 2 (1990): 175–89.

Huizinga, Johan. *Homo Ludens: A Study of the Play-Element in Culture.* Boston: Beacon Press, 1950.

Hunter, James Davison. *American Evangelicalism: Conservative Religion and the Quandary of Modernity.* New Brunswick, N.J., 1983.

Jackall, Robert. *Moral Mazes: The World of Corporate Managers.* New York: Oxford University Press, 1988.

Jacobs, Janet L. "Gender and Power in New Religious Movements: A Feminist Discourse on the Scientific Study of Religion." *Religion* 21 (1991): 345–56.

———. "Women-Centered Healing Rites: A Study of Alienation and Reintegration." In *In Gods We Trust: New Patterns of Religious Pluralism in America,* 2nd rev.ed., edited by Thomas Robbins and Dick Anthony, 373–84. New Brunswick, N.J.: Transaction Publishers, 1990.

Johnson, Frank A., and Douglas F. Zatzick. "Indigenous Psychotherapeutic Practices among Middle Class Americans: II. Some Conceptual and Practical Comparisons." Unpublished Paper. 1994.

Jones, Steven G. "Understanding Community in the Information Age." In *CyberSociety: Computer-Mediated Communication and Community,* edited by Steven G. Jones, 10–35. Thousand Oaks, Cal.: Sage Publications, 1995.

Joralemon, Donald. "The Selling of the Shaman and the Problem of

Informant Legitimacy." *Journal of Anthropological Research* 46, no. 2 (1990): 105–18.

Kaminer, Wendy. *I'm Dysfunctional, You're Dysfunctional: The Recovery Movement and Other Self-Help Fashions*. Reading, Mass.: Addison-Wesley, 1992.

———. "Feminism's Identity Crisis." *Atlantic Monthly*, October 1993, 51–68.

Katz, Jon. "Return of the Luddites." *Wired*, June 1995, 162–65, 210.

Kehoe, Alice B. "Prima Gaia: Primitivists and Plastic Medicine Men." In *The Invented Indian: Cultural Fictions and Government Policies*, edited by James M. Clifton, 193–209. New Brunswick, N.J.: Transaction Publishers, 1990.

Kelly, Kevin. "Embrace It." *Harper's Magazine*, May 1994, 20–25.

Kenny, Michael G. "Multiple Personality and Spirit Possession." *Psychiatry* 44 (1981): 337–58.

———. *The Passion of Anselm Bourne: Multiple Personality in American Culture*. Smithsonian Series in Ethnographic Inquiry. Washington, D.C.: Smithsonian Institution Press, 1986.

Kitch, Sally L. *Chaste Liberation: Celibacy and Female Cultural Status*. Urbana, Ill.: University of Illinois Press, 1989.

Klaw, Spencer. *Without Sin: The Life and Death of the Oneida Community*. New York: Allen Lane/Penguin, 1993.

Klimo, Jon. *Channeling: Investigations on Receiving Information from Paranormal Sources*. Los Angeles: Jeremy P. Tarcher, 1987.

Kosmin, Barry A., and Seymour P. Lachman. *One Nation Under God: Religion in Contemporary American Society*. New York: Crown, 1993.

Koteen, Judi Pope, ed. *Last Waltz of the Tyrants: The Prophecy*. Hillsboro, Ore.: Beyond Words Publishing, 1989.

Lambek, Michael. *Human Spirits: A Cultural Account of Trance in Mayotte*. New York: Cambridge University Press, 1981.

———. *Knowledge and Practice in Mayotte: Local Discourses of Islam, Sorcery, and Spirit Possession*. Toronto: University of Toronto Press, 1993.

Lemann, Nicholas. "Is There a Science of Success?" *Atlantic Monthly*, February 1994, 83–98.

Lenz, Elinor, and Barbara Myerhoff. *The Feminization of America: How Women's Values Are Changing Our Public and Private Lives.* Los Angeles: Jeremy P. Tarcher, 1985.

Lewis, I. M. *Ecstatic Religion: An Anthropological Study of Spirit Possession and Shamanism.* Harmondsworth: Penguin, 1971.

———. "What is a Shaman?" *Folk* 23 (1981): 25–35.

Lewis, James R. "Approaches to the Study of the New Age Movement." In *Perspectives on the New Age,* edited by James R. Lewis and J. Gordon Melton, 1–12. Albany: State University of New York Press, 1992.

Lifton, Robert Jay. *The Protean Self: Human Resilience in an Age of Fragmentation.* New York: Basic Books, 1993.

Luhrmann, T. M. *Persuasions of the Witch's Craft: Ritual Magic in Contemporary England.* Cambridge: Harvard University Press, 1989.

———. "The Resurgence of Romanticism: Contemporary Neopaganism, Feminist Spirituality and the Divinity of Nature." In *Environmentalism: The View from Anthropology,* edited by Kay Milton, 219–32. ASA Monograph 32. London: Routledge, 1993.

MacLaine, Shirley. *Out on a Limb.* New York: Bantam, 1983.

Manderscheid, Ronald W., and Mary Anne Sonnenschein, editors. *Mental Health, United States 1990.* National Institute of Mental Health, U.S. Department of Health and Human Services. Washington, D.C.: U.S. Government Printing Office, 1990.

Martin, Emily. "Health and Wealth in the U.S.A.." Paper presented at the International Congress of Anthropological and Ethnological Sciences. Quebec, Canada, 1983.

McLaughlin, Corine, and Gordon Davidson. *Builders of the Dawn: Community Lifestyles in a Changing World.* Summertown, Tenn.: Book Publishing Company, 1985.

McLoughlin, William G. *Revivals, Awakenings, and Reform: An Essay on Religion and Social Change in America, 1607–1977.* Chicago: University of Chicago Press, 1978.

Melton, J. Gordon. "Another Look at New Religions." In *Religion in the Nineties.,* edited by Wade Clark Roof, 97–112. Special issue of the *Annals of the American Academy of Political and Social Science,* Vol. 527, 1993.

———. "New Thought and the New Age." In *Perspectives on the New Age,* edited by James R. Lewis and J. Gordon Melton, 15–29. Albany: State University of New York Press, 1992.

Melton, J. Gordon, Jerome Clark, and Aidan A. Kelly. *New Age Encyclopedia.* Detroit, Mich.: Gale Research, 1990.

Merrill, William L., Edmund J. Ladd, and T. J. Ferguson. "The Return of the Ahayu:da: Lessons for Repatriation from Zuni Pueblo and the Smithsonian Institution." *Current Anthropology* 34, no. 5 (1993): 523–67.

Merskey, H. "The Manufacture of Personalities: The Production of Multiple Personality Disorder." *British Journal of Psychiatry* 160 (1992): 327–40.

Meyer, Donald. *The Positive Thinkers: Religion as Pop Psychology from Mary Baker Eddy to Oral Roberts.* New York: Pantheon, 1980.

Moore, R. Laurence. *In Search of White Crows: Spiritualism, Psychology and American Culture.* New York: Oxford University Press, 1977.
———. *Selling God: American Religion in the Marketplace of Culture.* New York: Oxford University Press, 1994.

Nathan, Debbie. "Dividing to Conquer?: Women, Men, and the Making of Multiple Personality Disorder." *Social Text* 40 (1994): 77–114.

Nietzel, Michael T., Douglas A. Bernstein, and Richard Milich. *Introduction to Clinical Psychology,* 3rd edition. Englewood Cliffs, N.J.: Prentice Hall, 1991.

Neitz, Mary Jo. "In Goddess We Trust." In *In Gods We Trust: New Patterns of Religious Pluralism in America,* 2nd rev. ed., edited by Thomas Robbins and Dick Anthony, 353–72. New Brunswick, N.J.: Transaction Publishers, 1990.

Nelson, Geoffrey K. *Spiritualism and Society.* New York: Schocken Books, 1969.

Oakes, Guy. *The Soul of the Salesman: The Moral Ethos of Personal Sales.* Atlantic Highlands, N.J.: Humanities Press International, 1990.

Owen, Alex. *The Darkened Room: Women, Power, and Spiritualism in Late Victorian England.* Philadelphia: University of Pennsylvania Press, 1990.

Palmer, Susan Jean. *Moon Sisters, Krishna Mothers, Rajneesh Lovers: Women's Roles in New Religions.* Syracuse, N.Y.: Syracuse University Press, 1994.

———. "Women's 'Cocoon Work' in New Religious Movements: Sexual Experimentation and Feminine Rites of Passage." *Journal for the Scientific Study of Religion* 32, no. 4 (1993): 343–55.

Parry, Jonathan P., and Maurice Bloch. "Introduction: Money and the Morality of Exchange." In *Money and the Morality of Exchange,* edited by Jonathan P. Parry and Maurice Bloch, 1–32. Cambridge: Cambridge University Press, 1989.

Peters, Larry G., and Douglass Price-Williams. "Towards an Experiential Analysis of Shamanism." *American Ethnologist* 7, no. 3 (1980): 397–418.

Petersen-Lowary, Sheila. *The Fifth Dimension: Channels to a New Reality.* New York: Fireside, 1988.

Pfeffer, Leo. "The Legitimation of Marginal Religions in the United States." In *Religious Movements in Contemporary America,* edited by Irving I. Zaretsky and Mark P. Leone, 9–26. Princeton, N.J.: Princeton University Press, 1974.

Philipson, Ilene J. *On the Shoulders of Women: The Feminization of Psychotherapy.* New York: Guilford Press, 1993.

Pickering, Sir George. *Creative Malady: Illness in the Lives and Minds of Charles Darwin, Florence Nightingale, Mary Baker Eddy, Sigmund Freud, Marcel Proust, Elizabeth Barrett Browning.* New York: Oxford University Press, 1974.

Press, Irwin. "The Urban Curandero." *American Anthropologist* 73 (1971): 742–56.

Prothero, Stephen. "From Spiritualism to Theosophy: 'Uplifting' a Democratic Tradition." *Religion and American Culture* 3, no. 2 (1993): 197–216.

Putnam, Robert D. "Bowling Alone: America's Declining Social Capital." *Journal of Democracy* 6, no. 1 (1995): 65–78.

Rheingold, Howard. *The Virtual Community: Homesteading on the Electronic Frontier.* Reading, Mass.: Addison-Wesley, 1993.

Richardson, James T., ed. *Money and Power in the New Religions.* Lewiston, N.Y.: Edwin Mellen Press, 1988.

Ridall, Kathryn. *Channeling: How to Reach Out to Your Spirit Guides.* New York: Bantam, 1988.

Rieff, Philip. *The Triumph of the Therapeutic: Uses of Faith After Freud.* New York: Harper & Row, 1966.

Riordan, Suzanne. "Channeling." In *New Age Encyclopedia,* J. Gordon Melton et al., 97–104. Detroit, Mich.: Gale Research, 1990.

———. "Channeling: A New Revelation?" In *Perspectives on the New Age,* edited by James R. Lewis and J. Gordon Melton, 105–26. Albany, N.Y.: State University of New York Press, 1992.

Robbins, Thomas, and David G. Bromley. "What Have We Learned About New Religions?: New Religious Movements as Experiments." *Religious Studies Review* 19, no. 3 (1993): 209–16.

Roberts, Jane. *The Seth Material.* Englewood Cliffs, N.J.: Prentice-Hall, 1970.

———. *Seth Speaks: The Eternal Validity of the Soul.* New York: Bantam, 1972.

Roberts, Marjory. "A Linguistic 'Nay' to Channeling." *Psychology Today,* October 1989, 64–65.

Rogers, Rayna L. "Multiple Personality and Channeling." *Jefferson Journal of Psychiatry* 9, no. 1 (1991): 3–13.

Roof, Wade Clark. *A Generation of Seekers: The Spiritual Journeys of the Baby Boom Generation.* San Francisco: HarperSanFrancisco, 1993.

Root, Deborah. *Cannibal Culture: Art, Appropriation, and the Commodification of Difference.* Boulder, Colo.: Westview, 1996.

Rose, Wendy. "The Great Pretenders: Further Reflections on White-shamanism." In *The State of Native America: Genocide, Colonization, and Resistance,* edited by M. Annette Jaimes, 403–21. Boston: South End Press, 1992.

Ross, Andrew. *Strange Weather: Culture, Science, and Technology in the Age of Limits.* London: Verso, 1991.

Ross, Colin A. "Twelve Cognitive Errors About Multiple Personality Disorder." *American Journal of Psychotherapy* 44, no. 3 (1990).

———"Epidemiology of Multiple Personality Disorder and Dissociation." *Psychiatric Clinics of North America* 14, no. 3 (1991): 503–16.

Rossman, Michael. *New Age Blues: On the Politics of Consciousness.* New York: E. P. Dutton, 1979.

Rupert, Glenn A. "Employing the New Age: Training Seminars." In *Perspectives on the New Age,* edited by James R. Lewis and J. Gordon Melton, 127–35. Albany: State University of New York Press, 1992.

Ryerson, Kevin, and Stephanie Harolde. *Spirit Communication: The Soul's Path.* New York: Bantam, 1989.

Schaefer, Stacy B. "Huichols, the New Age Movement, and the Native American Church: Ethical Considerations in Long-Term Fieldwork." Paper presented at Annual Meeting of the American Anthropological Association, 1993.

Schapiro, Barbara. "From Narcissism to the New Spiritualism: Reflections on the New Age." *Cimarron Review* 91 (April 1990): 72–82.

Schur, Edwin. *The Awareness Trap: Self-Absorption Instead of Social Change.* New York: McGraw-Hill, 1976.

Schwartz, Hillel. *Century's End: A Cultural History of the Fin de Siècle from the 990s through the 1990s.* New York: Doubleday, 1990.

Sherrill, Rowland A. "Recovering American Religious Sensibility: An Introduction." In *Religion and the Life of the Nation: American Recoveries,* edited by Rowland A. Sherrill, 1–22. Urbana, Ill.: University of Illinois Press, 1990.

Simmel, Georg. *The Philosophy of Money.* Translated by Tom Bottomore and David Frisby. London: Routledge and Kegan Paul, 1978 [orig. 1907].

Skultans, Vieda. *Intimacy and Ritual: A Study of Spiritualism, Mediums, and Groups.* London: Routledge and Kegan Paul, 1974.

Smith, Andrea. "For All Those Who Were Indian in a Former Life." *Cultural Survival Quarterly* 17, no. 4 (1994): 70–71.

Sontag, Susan. *Illness as Metaphor.* New York: Farrar, Straus, and Giroux, 1978.

Spanos, Nicholas P., John R. Weekes, and Lorne D. Bertrand. "Multiple Personality: A Social Psychological Perspective." *Journal of Abnormal Psychology* 94, no. 3 (1985): 362–76.

Spiegel, David, and Etzel Cardeña. "Disintegrated Experience: The

Dissociative Disorders Revisted." *Journal of Abnormal Psychology* 100, no. 3 (1991): 366–78.

Stacey, Judith. *Brave New Families: Tales of Domestic Upheaval in Late Twentieth Century America.* New York: Basic Books, 1991.

Stark, Rodney. "Europe's Receptivity to New Religious Movements: Round Two." *Journal for the Scientific Study of Religion* 32, no. 4 (1993): 389–97.

Stevens, José, and Simon Warwick-Smith. *The Michael Handbook.* Orinda, Cal.: Warwick Press, 1988.

Stifler, Kenneth, Joanne Greer, William Sneck, and Robert Dovenmuehle. "An Empirical Investigation of the Discriminability of Reported Mystical Experiences among Religious Contemplatives, Psychotic Inpatients, and Normal Adults." *Journal for the Scientific Study of Religion* 32, no. 4 (1993): 366–72.

Talbott, Stephen L. *The Future Does Not Compute: Transcending the Machines in Our Midst.* Sebastapol, Cal.: O'Reilly and Associates, 1995.

Tart, Charles T. "A Systems Approach to Altered States of Consciousness." In *The Psychobiology of Consciousness,* edited by Julian M. Davidson and Richard J. Davidson, 243–69. New York: Plenum, 1980.

Taylor, Charles. *Sources of the Self: The Making of Modern Identity.* Cambridge, Mass.: Harvard University Press, 1989.

Taylor, Mark C. *Disfiguring: Art, Architecture, Religion.* Chicago: University of Chicago Press, 1992.

———, and Esa Saarinen. *Imagologies: Media Philosophy.* London: Routledge, 1994.

Thomason, Sarah Grey. "'Entities' in the Linguistic Minefield." *Skeptical Inquirer* 13 (1989): 391–96.

Tipton, Steven M. *Getting Saved from the Sixties: Moral Meaning in Conversion and Cultural Change.* Berkeley: University of California Press, 1982.

Tocqueville, Alexis de. *Democracy in America.* Edited by J. P. Mayer. Garden City, N.Y.: Anchor, 1969 [orig. 1835].

Turkle, Sherry. *Life on the Screen: Identity in the Age of the Internet.* New York: Simon and Schuster, 1995.

Turner, Victor W. *The Drums of Affliction: A Study of Religious Processes among the Ndembu of Zambia*. Oxford: Clarendon Press and The International African Institute, 1968.

W., Lynn, ed. *Mending Ourselves: Expressions of Healing and Self-Integration*. Cincinnati, Oh.: Many Voices Press, 1993.

Wagenheim, Jeff. "Among the Promise Keepers." *New Age Journal,* March/April 1995, 78–81; 126–30.

Winkelman, Michael. "Trance States: A Theoretical Model and Cross-Cultural Analysis." *Ethos* 14 (1986): 174–203.

Woodhouse, Annie. *Fantastic Women: Sex, Gender and Transvestism*. New Brunswick, N.J.: Rutgers University Press, 1989.

Wuthnow, Robert. *Meaning and Moral Order: Explorations in Cultural Analysis*. Berkeley: University of California Press, 1987.

———. *Sharing the Journey: Support Groups and America's Quest for Community*. New York: The Free Press, 1994.

Yarbro, Chelsea Q. *Messages from Michael*. New York: Simon & Schuster, 1979.

Zaretsky, Irving I. "In the Beginning Was the Word: The Relationship of Language to Social Organization in Spiritualist Churches." In *Religious Movements in Contemporary America,* edited by Irving I. Zaretsky and Mark P. Leone, 166–219. Princeton: Princeton University Press, 1974.

———, and Mark P. Leone, eds. *Religious Movements in Contemporary America*. Princeton: Princeton University Press, 1974.

Zatzick, Douglas F., and Frank A. Johnson. "Indigenous Psychotherapeutic Practices among Middle Class Americans: I. Case Studies and Follow-up." Unpublished paper, 1994.

INDEX

Aguaruna Indians, 76–77, 79, 80
Affirmations, 143, 150
Altered states of consciousness, 6, 19–21, 175, 199n5; and mental illness, 19–20. *See also* Dissociation
Alternative therapies, 7, 188; relationship to institutional religion, 173
American Indians. *See* Native Americans
Analytical reason, channels' critique of, 26, 29, 42
Androgyny, 101, 103–105, 111, 113–114
Angels, 5, 6, 14, 87, 98. *See also* Archangel Gabriel; Entities
Apocalyptic prophecies, 5, 43–44, 127, 186
Archangel Gabriel, 21, 132–135, 186
Ascended Masters, 4, 23, 25, 74, 86, 105–106, 108, 130
Atun-Re (spirit), 28–29. *See also* Ryerson, Kevin
Authenticity, search for, 178
Azande, 67

Baby Boom generation, 7; religious attitudes, 91, 139, 172–173, 209n14; occupational anxieties, 150–151
Bailey, Alice, 72, 156
Ballard, Guy, 105–106
Bellah, Robert N., 139
Blavatsky, Helena Petrovna, 23, 156. *See also* Theosophy
Body, as source of wisdom, 42
Bourguignon, Erika, 205n3
Branch Davidians, 127
Braun, Bennett G., 181

Cayce, Edgar, 6, 193
Channelers. *See* Channels
Channeling sessions: humor, 29, 43; social dynamics, 30, 79–80, 119–123, 134–135; linguistic features, 31–32, 79–80, 133, 200nn12, 13; sex ratio, 71, 95, 99; interactive elements, 84, 86
Channels: estimated number in U.S., 6; social background, 7–8; and gender, 11, 93–114; ethics, 64–65, 85; sex ratio, 95, 206n4; gay and lesbian, 103, 171; relations with clients, 122–123, 153–155; intellectual curiosity of, 123, 186; attitudes toward money, 153–155

11, 94–95, 97–98, 112;
attracted to channeling, 11,
95–102, 112–114, 117, 165;
spiritual inclinations of, 95–101;
and multiple personality, 181,
182–183. *See also* Androgyny;
Feminism

Wounded healer, power of, 57
Wuthnow, Robert, 140, 143

Xavier, Chico, 81

Zuni Indians, 166–167, 212n16